HOW TO DESIGN AND BUILD YOUR GARDEN RAILROAD

by Jack Verducci

KALMBACH BOOKS

Dedicated to my partner in the railroad, in the garden, and in my life—my wife, Pauline.

Printed in the United States of America

06 07 08 09 10 11 12 13 14 15   10 9 8 7 6 5 4 3 2 1

Visit our Web site at
http://kalmbachbooks.com
Secure online ordering available

ISBN-10: 0-89024-664-5
ISBN-13: 978-0-89024-664-1

Publisher's Cataloging-In-Publication Data
(Prepared by The Donohue Group, Inc.)

Verducci, Jack.
  How to design and build your garden railroad / by Jack Verducci.

    p. : ill. ; cm.

  "The material in this book has previously appeared as articles in Garden Railways magazine."
  ISBN-13: 978-0-89024-644-3
  ISBN-10: 0-89024-644-0

1. Railroads--Models. 2. Railroads--Models--Design and construction. I. Title. II. Title: Garden railways.

TF197 .V47 2006
625.1/9

The material in this book has previously appeared as articles in *Garden Railways* magazine.

Contents

About the author

Jack Verducci has always had an interest in models and miniatures. As a child, he built ship, automobile, and train models. He built his first layout (HO scale) in the early 1960s as a Boy Scout project with his brother. He discovered large-scale trains during his time in the Navy in the late '60s, after purchasing a Märklin starter set.

In 1988, he built the initial version of his Crystal Springs Railroad, and displayed it at the fifth National Garden Railroad Convention in the summer of 1989. A few years later, in 1992, Jack began building garden railroads professionally. Since that time, he has built nearly 75 garden railroads in many areas of the country, as well as a few indoor layouts. He recently earned the National Model Railroad Association's title of Master Model Railroader based on his garden-railroad accomplishments. Jack is also a regular contributor to *Garden Railways* magazine. His "Garden railway design & construction" column has appeared regularly in the magazine since December 1996.

Jack lives in the San Francisco Bay area in California with his wife, Pauline. In his spare time, he enjoys sailing his boat with Pauline, his two sons, and their families.

Introduction

Welcome to garden railroading, a wonderful outdoor hobby that the entire family can enjoy! There's something for everyone's interests, including gardening and landscaping, electronics, model building, and running trains. The challenge for many folks is taking that first step and breaking ground for a garden railway.

There are many challenges in building a garden line, such as establishing the grade and digging a pond. Before you christen that shovel, however, you'll need to develop a vision for your dream railroad. What type of railroad interests you—running steam locomotives through Colorado or operating modern-day diesels in Chicago?

Theme

One major element distinguishes a great garden railway from a mediocre one: a theme. A garden-railway theme usually includes an era, a geographical location, the type of railroad, and a certain scale and gauge.

You can model whatever geological area interests you. Dorothy Barr was interested in Swiss railroads. Her garden line reflects that area using mountains, forest trees, and stonework.

Miniature landscaping has value beyond its use with a railroad. Even without a train, this mountain area is a beautiful setting, especially when viewed from inside the house (at right).

Working within a theme helps establish continuity and a sense of purpose for your railroad. For example, if you decide to model a 1920s-era narrow gauge railroad located in the mining areas of the Colorado Rockies, you will want trains, automobiles, buildings, and details from that time period. If you want to have several themes, the railroad can be broken into sections, each featuring a different theme. You also can have a railroad with no theme. It means your theme is "anything goes," and that's fine, too.

The elements of a theme

Era

An era is a period of time considered in terms of noteworthy and characteristic events and developments. Examples include the Civil War, westward expansion, the Great Depression, the diesel era, and the modern era.

For my Crystal Springs Railroad, I decided to model 1939. With this decision, I made an effort to learn more about that period. I started collecting books and articles with photos taken during this time. Staying within an era requires discipline, which sometimes may be difficult. For example, no matter how much you love that 1957 Thunderbird, it obviously would be out of place in a Depression-era railroad.

Geographical location and miniature landscaping

If you like the mountains, you may want to re-create them in miniature as part of your garden railway. You can choose from an unlimited number of real locations for landscaping motifs such as the desert, the ocean shore, a riverfront, and the prairies. You can combine as many of these imaginary locations as you like into your railroad landscape. Sometimes the imaginary location will be dictated by the site on which you are building. In my case, mountain railroading was a natural for part of my railroad. I was able to use the natural grade in my yard to advantage in creating a coastal range and a logging camp.

A freight train led by double-headed live-steam locomotives makes its way up the Pacific Coast Range on the author's Crystal Springs Railroad.

Miniature landscaping has value beyond its use as a railroad setting. It can be used as a sight block, for example, to hide a fence or a neighbor's house. It can also become a backdrop for full-size landscaping.

Even without a train, the miniature landscape can be used to create the illusion of vast space in a small area. I believe the landscaping is the most important visual part of a garden railroad because that is what you see every time you look out the window.

Type of railroad

The type of railroad includes examples such as mining railroads, logging railroads, and mill railroads. You also can include a traction line as a type of railway. You do not have to limit yourself to just one type. My Crystal Springs Railroad is a general-purpose common carrier. A series of small industrial railroads delivers goods to the CSRR interchange tracks, plus I have a small traction (electric railroad) line.

Gauge

Gauge is the distance between the rails. The real Union Pacific, for example, is a standard gauge railroad, meaning the rails are 4 feet, 8½ inches apart. The Durango & Silverton Railroad, in Colorado, is a narrow gauge railroad; its gauge is three feet. The Monson Railroad in Maine is also a narrow gauge railroad, but with a gauge of two feet.

Scale

Scale is the size of a model compared to its prototype. If you are modeling in 1:32 scale, the model is ⅟₃₂ the size of the real thing. 1:32 is expressed as a ratio. Another way to express scale is as a fraction: for example, ⅟₃₂.

The issue of scale versus track gauge has long been a source of confusion. The most common track used outdoors, Gauge 1 (also called No. 1 Gauge), has rails 45mm apart. It's one of several model railroad gauges that have been around for decades. Rather than inventing a new

A water feature adds a dramatic element to a garden railroad. Here Shay locomotive No. 3 crosses a bridge with a string of logging cars on the Crystal Springs Lumber Company line.

gauge, manufacturers make equipment in several scales to run on Gauge 1 track. Although this equipment will run on the same track, this does not mean it is prototypically correct for your chosen scale. Generally, if you are using Gauge 1 track and running standard gauge equipment, the correct scale is 1:32. If you are using the same track and running three-foot narrow gauge, the correct scale is 1:20.3. See the sidebar below for more information.

Modes of operation

In general, garden railroads are run by one of three different kinds of operators: engineer, dispatcher, or observer.

The engineer runs the train, either following it with a remote-control unit or running it from a fixed point. The best real-life example of the engineer concept is a manually controlled live-steam operation. The engineer must stay with the engine, minding the water and fuel levels and steam pressure. With electrically powered trains, speed is the primary concern of the engineer. The engineer often acts as the switch operator, too, throwing the turnouts to route the train. In other words, the operator of the train is mobile and interactive.

Popular scale equipment manufactured for use on Gauge 1 track

Scale	Prototype
1:13.7 (⅞")	two-foot narrow gauge
1:20.3	three-foot narrow gauge
1:22.5	European meter gauge
1:24	42" gauge
1:29	Used by some manufacturers as standard gauge
1:32	Standard gauge

Fred Feltner's railroad, in San Jose, California, features this beautiful trestle, built by the author using the methods described in Chapter 1.

The dispatcher sits at a central control panel from which he or she operates the trains. By means of remotely controlled turnouts and blocks, the trains are routed around the railroad. Except for an occasional need to clean up an accident, the dispatcher remains stationary while operating trains.

The observer is a person who sits somewhere along the line, watching the trains go by. This is easily accomplished by having one or more main lines set up to run one train each or by using automatic block controls. In this case, the trains are self-sufficient. An operator is necessary only to start the system and correct any malfunctions.

Type of operation should be a factor in designing your railroad. If you have an area where access is limited, you may want to use the dispatcher concept so you don't have to walk to each turnout. If you have a very large area that cannot be seen from one spot, you may want to be an observer and let the trains run automatically. The choice is up to you.

Types of track plans

There are a variety of basic track plans you can choose from when you plan a garden railway. For some basic examples, see the sidebar on page 10.

Don't be intimidated

I have presented a lot of information for you to consider. Don't think you have to make decisions on everything before you start your railroad. I didn't. It's amazing how things will change as you actually start building. Be prepared to change. More often than not, elaborately drawn plans have to be modified when you actually put them in practice. Don't be afraid of making a mistake, and above all, have fun!

BASIC LARGE-SCALE TRACK PLANS

Basic continuous-run track plans

Trains using these track plans follow a single route and require no special operation to run.

The **loop** is the most basic of track plans for continuous running, and it can be any shape. What makes a loop attractive is that the train can run forever without coming to the end of the track. The loop can be expanded and made more interesting by the addition of passing sidings, spurs, and branch lines. With the addition of landscaping, the basic loop can be further enhanced.

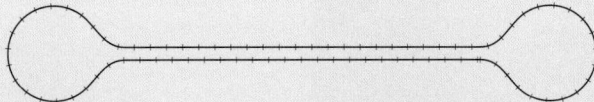

The **dogbone** is similar to the basic loop except that there is a loop at each end to turn the train around. Between the loops, the train runs on what appears to be a double track. This plan works well in flower beds where there may not be enough room for turns in the center areas, but where there is room at the ends or corners.

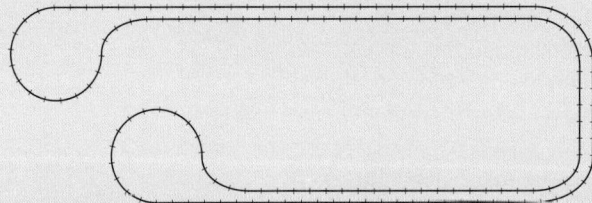

The **folded dogbone** is the same as the dogbone, but the track is arranged to fit into a specific area. Dogbones can also be folded and twisted to create situations where the train passes over and under itself. We will see this versatile plan used in the future.

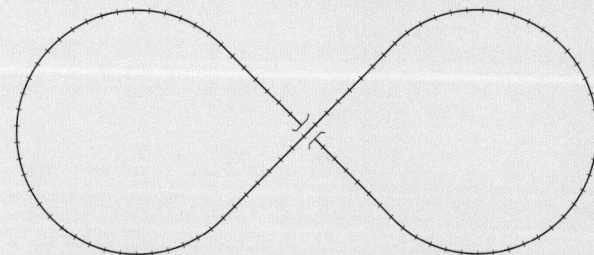

The **figure-eight, over-and-under** is one of my favorite track plans for small areas. A basic figure-eight can also be built on a single level by using a crossing track. However, a more interesting figure-eight is one that goes over and under itself. With this plan, when you include a bridge or a tunnel, the train appears to be running on two levels. I've built railways in areas as small as 8 x 16 feet using a figure-eight. In spite of its small size, I was still able to include a tunnel, a bridge, a small switch yard, and a mining branch line. Most large-scale locomotives can pull trains of three or four cars up and over the necessary grade.

Point-to-point track plans

Trains using these track plans run to the end, then return by backing up. Other options include using a turntable, wye, passing siding, or reversing loop.

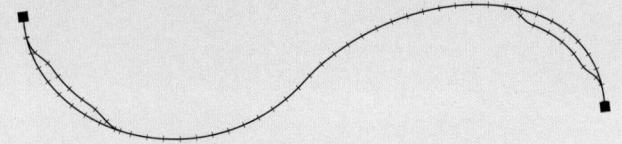

The **point-to-point,** in its basic form, runs from one end of the line to the other without the locomotive turning around. This plan can be improved by adding a passing siding at each end. The engineer can park the cars on the mainline (at a station), then bring the locomotive around the train and couple it to the other end for the return trip.

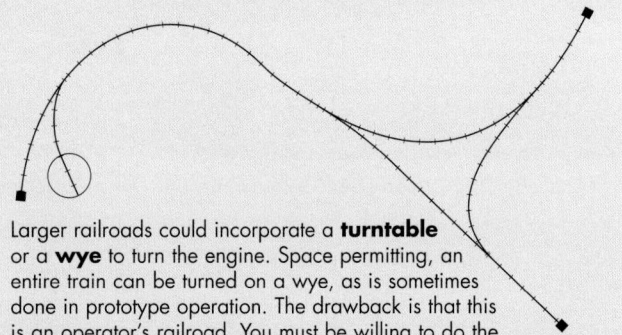

Larger railroads could incorporate a **turntable** or a **wye** to turn the engine. Space permitting, an entire train can be turned on a wye, as is sometimes done in prototype operation. The drawback is that this is an operator's railroad. You must be willing to do the switching at each end. This is for people who like the engineer philosophy of operation.

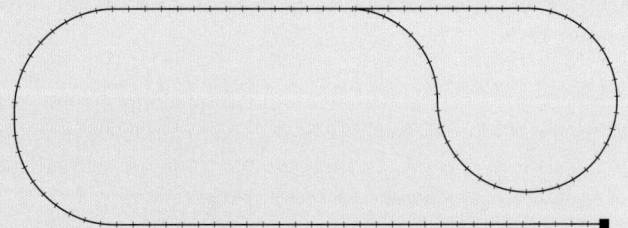

The **point-to-loop plan** allows a train to go from one point to another on a single track, then to turn around for the return trip without a switching maneuver. At the "point" end (the end without the loop), the train could again be turned on a turntable or wye. This plan could be used in an area where you have room to turn at one end of the line but not at the other. Using the engineer concept of operation, you could have a switch yard at the "point" end, where cars could be made up into a train that would then be sent out to the loop end, where it would be turned for the return trip.

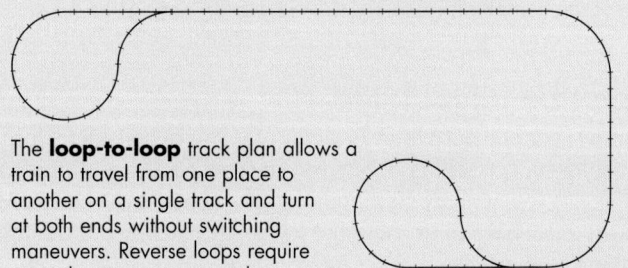

The **loop-to-loop** track plan allows a train to travel from one place to another on a single track and turn at both ends without switching maneuvers. Reverse loops require special wiring to prevent short circuits and should be used only if absolutely necessary.

CHAPTER 1

Choosing the perfect place

Denise Pitsch's line (designed and built by the author) in Palo Alto, California, is a simple figure-eight track plan with a passing siding, some spurs, and a separate mining line— a lot of action for an 8 x 16-foot space.

Perhaps you're starting to develop an idea of the kind of garden railway you'd like. Before you make a final decision, choose a site and survey the area. These steps will help you determine where things should go, how you will get materials in, what utilities you'll need, and where you'll want to run your roadbed.

Site selection, surveying, and layout

Site selection

Site selection and a survey go hand in hand. You must choose a site, then survey it to see if it will work. In a small yard, you may have little choice as to where to put the railroad. For a larger lot, here are a few things to consider.

I believe that the worst terrain makes the best site for a garden railway. A hillside or rough area makes an excellent railroad site. The idea of taking an otherwise useless section of land and developing it into a beautiful miniature landscape is an interesting and challenging undertaking. So keep in mind parts of your property that are not presently developed and that you may have written off.

Another consideration is whether or not you want to see the railway from your house. In some cases, you'll be able to create a spectacular view from your window.

Look for hidden assets. Taking a different look at things often reveals a natural feature that you already have in your yard, one that can be enhanced and used in your railroad's landscaping. For example, you may have an area that has suffered some erosion. This could be used as a dry wash, a draw, or a valley.

You may be fortunate enough to have a stream or creek that you can run the track next to or over.

Surveying

Once you have decided on a basic track plan, you can lay it out in three dimensions right in its proposed space. A three-dimensional plan is far superior to anything you can do on paper because you will be able to see exactly where the train will run. The method I will show you here can be used to prove your drawings or to create a track plan from scratch, without the use of a drawn plan. In addition to allowing you to see the actual path of the track, it will also allow you to easily make changes and adjustments.

Drawing an accurate track plan for a garden railway can take almost as much time as building the actual railroad. Some people have problems converting three-dimensional ideas into two-dimensional drawings. I have used the system described below for many years and it works, replacing the need to do drawings on paper.

I have discovered that ½" schedule 40 PVC pipe behaves much like flex-track, so I use it to represent the track. I use wooden stakes to lay out the grade. You must first survey your site to locate the existing hills and valleys. Once you have your site survey, you can proceed with the track plan. As an example here, I am using a figure-eight, over-and-under track plan. Starting at the

lowest point, which can be called "ground zero," lay out the track plan using PVC pipe as track. There is no need to glue the pipe joints. The pipe can be curved very closely to the shape you want, and it will hold that position (within reason) once all the pipes are connected. At this point, don't worry if the pipe is not placed exactly. Next, lay out wooden stakes every five feet along the proposed roadbed. Then, drive the stakes into the ground. The stakes will do two things: They will be used to determine the track elevation, and they will hold the PVC pipe in place.

Next, determine if there is a significant grade and what that grade is. There are several ways of doing this. The professional way is with a builder's sight level or transit, which can be rented. The device is used to measure elevation changes (**fig. 1**).

A transit is especially useful on large, rough plots. For smaller areas, or areas with relatively flat terrain, a mason's string level can be used. These cost about two dollars at a hardware store. This method is more primitive, but still effective (**fig. 2**).

In either case, the grade is determined by measuring from the sight line or the string line at selected points. Start at the lowest point and note the elevation. Then go to the highest spot and do the same. The vertical distance is the difference between these two points. Divide the difference in elevation by the running distance between the two

The stakes here will be used to determine track elevation and to keep the PVC pipe in place. If a stake is driven too far down, add a second piece of wood set to the correct height.

Using PVC pipe as a three-dimensional track plan works well with complex designs. It helps visualize where things are to be placed, and can also serve as a construction guide.

points to determine the percentage of overall grade.

Figuring grade

In a figure-eight track plan (or any type of track plan where one track crosses over another), a minimum of 9" of clearance is needed below the upper track (12" is better). Check this clearance for your railroad by measuring the height of your tallest piece of rolling stock and adding the thickness of the bridge you will be using. (Your locomotives are not necessarily the tallest—cabooses are often taller.)

Now that you know the clearance height, you can calculate the grade. Let's say you need 12" of clearance and you have a figure-eight with two loops, each 12 feet across. You need to determine the length of the track, starting from ground zero up to the crossover point. Use π (pi, or 3.14) to determine that distance. The formula is: π x diameter = circumference (πd = c). In our example, 3.14 (π) x 12 (diameter) = 37.68 feet (the circumference of each loop). This means we have about 37.5 feet in which to climb 12". Figure the grade by converting 37.5 feet into inches (12 x 37.5 = 450), then dividing the height (12) by the distance (450): 12 ÷ 450 = .026, or 2.6 percent (approximately 3 percent).

Setting the stakes

Once the grade is known, the wooden grade stakes can be set to the proper height. I space mine 60" apart, so a 3 percent grade would be about 1¾" of rise or fall between stakes. Starting at ground zero, set each consecutive stake 1¾" higher than the previous one until the crossover is reached, then do the reverse, setting each consecutive stake 1¾" lower than the one before. I use 60" because that spacing works well to support the 10-foot lengths of PVC pipe. (If I spaced the stakes 8 feet apart, the rise and fall would be very close to 1" = 1 percent. While this would be easier for calculating the grade, I like the stakes closer together for support purposes. The chart at the bottom of page 14 provides some quick grade calculations based on 60" spacing.

Setting the stakes to grade can be done in several ways. One is to hammer

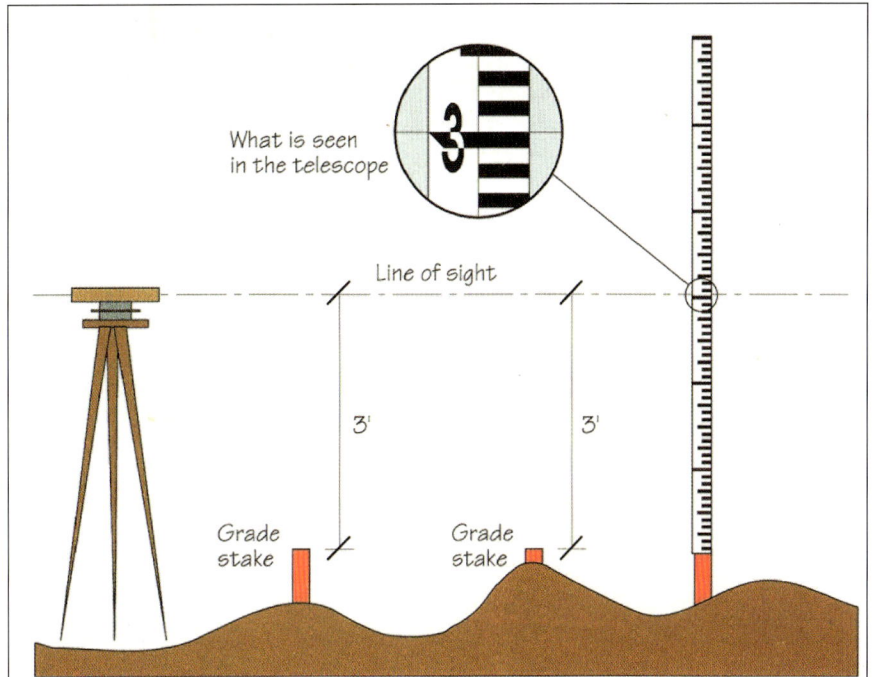

Fig. 1 – Determining grade using a transit
A sight level or transit works like a mason's string level, except that the line is invisible. Elevation is read through the crosshairs in the telescope, which is leveled on a platform. A second person holds a measuring stick from which the reading is taken. The grade is determined as shown in fig. 2. Advantages to using a transit are that there is no string to worry about, the method is very accurate, and you can measure over a large field without having to continually reset equipment. In the above example, a level grade is being laid.

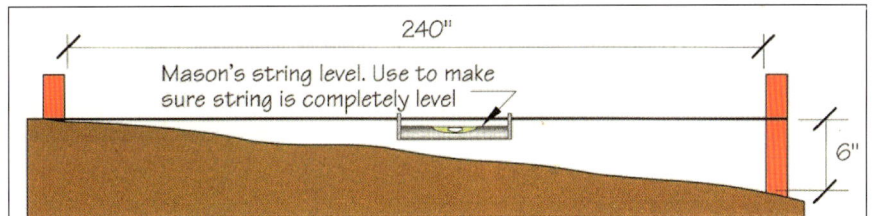

Fig. 2a – Determining grade using a string level
In this illustration, the run is 240" between the stakes, with a 6" difference in elevation measured at the ground. To determine the grade, divide the difference in elevation (6") by the distance (240"): 6 ÷ 240 = .025, or 2.5 percent.

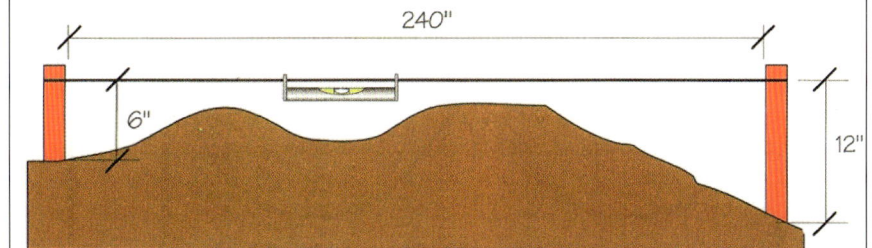

Fig. 2b – Determining ultimate grade over uneven ground
When working with uneven ground, the string must be raised to clear obstacles. Compute the actual elevation difference by subtracting the lesser from the greater. In this example, the elevation difference is 6". Figure the grade the same way as shown in fig. 2a.

the stake down to the correct height. If the ground is hard, however, you can hammer the stake down far enough to ensure that it is firmly anchored, then mark the correct height and cut the stake at that point. Another method is to pound the stake in below grade, then attach a second piece of wood to the main stake at the correct setting, screwing that piece to the stake.

When this is done, you will have a series of grade stakes properly set that will represent the elevation along the future right-of-way. Screw the PVC pipe to the grade stakes to create your three-dimensional track plan.

I generally leave the stakes in the ground forever; you certainly need to leave them in place throughout the project. If you need to temporarily remove the pipe for access, simply unscrew it, then replace it when you are done. If you remove the pipe, flag the grade stake so that if you inadvertently cover it up, you can find it later. Now that the grade and track plan are laid out in three dimensions, you can design landscaping and water features.

A hypothetical railroad

Unless you are building a flatland railroad, you probably will want to incorporate elevation and landscaping through which your railroad can run. A simple and effective way to do this in a relatively small, flat area is with a figure-eight track plan. This plan can be altered and embellished in many ways, but for now we'll stick to the basics.

Using your site drawing, determine how much room you have to fit the figure-eight. My philosophy regarding curves is to make them as broad as possible. If your area is 20 feet wide, use a 10-foot-radius curve. If you have only eight feet, still make the radius as broad as will fit. I'm a strong believer in flextrack and wouldn't use anything else. This provides the freedom to make gentle, sweeping curves of any radius.

Suppose we are working with a basically flat space measuring 19 x 20 feet. We must assume that a theme and style for the railway has already been

In the background is the mining railroad's trestle. In front is the mainline bridge and transfer facility. A compact rail yard and town can be seen under the bridge, and a small mountain lake is just to the left. This entire railroad is elevated 12" from ground level.

Useful information for placing grade stakes

I place grade stakes 5 feet (60") apart. At this spacing, 10-foot lengths of PVC pipe are firmly supported. Equal spacing makes calculating linear distance easy; you just count the sections and multiply by 5 feet. The chart below lists the heights needed to achieve the desired grade.

Rise or fall between stakes based on 60" spacing

Percent of grade	Rise or fall between stakes	
	Exact	Nominal
1.0%	0.6"	½"
1.5%	0.9"	1"
2.0%	1.2"	1¼"
2.5%	1.5"	1½"
3.0%	1.8"	1¾"
3.5%	2.1"	2"

Formula to figure circumference of a circle

π (pi) = 3.14

π x diameter = circumference

Circumferences for some common Gauge 1 railroad curves

2' radius (LGB no. 1100)
4' diameter = 12.56' circumference

3' radius (LGB no. 1500)
6' diameter = 18.84' circumference

4' radius (LGB no. 1600)
8' diameter = 25.12' circumference

5' radius
10' diameter = 31.4' circumference

6' radius
12' diameter =37.6' circumference

10' radius
20' diameter = 62.8' circumference

11' radius
22' diameter = 96.08' circumference

Mainline grades

On a main line, 2 percent or less is the recommended maximum grade for the best overall performance. In the real world, though, this cannot always be achieved. You can run a short train of three to six cars (depending on their size and weight) on a 3.5 percent grade without problem.

chosen. For this example, we want a mountain, a small lake, and a waterfall.

A figure-eight that is completely exposed looks toylike. To create the illusion that the train is traveling somewhere, plan a tunnel at one end of the railway. This will disguise the turn and block the train from view as it comes around the curve, which will add to the illusion that the train is changing direction. It's fun to watch the train disappear and reappear. Two tunnels on a small railroad might be too much, but built-up rock formations could be used to partially hide the curve at one end.

We first raise the area by installing a row of boulders around the perimeter to bring the lowest point up by 12". Some space will be lost in doing this, so a 12" margin will be designed around the area. The boulders may not actually fill the margin, but we will use the space inside it for the purposes of track planning. If there is room left over, we can always expand the curves a little.

The next step is to determine what the track grade will be. In order for the track to cross over itself, a rise of 10.5" will be required to allow clearance beneath the bridge. (Since this is a small railroad, small equipment will be used. On a larger line with bigger rolling stock, more clearance may be required.) Calculate the circumference of the eight-foot-diameter circle using the formula $\pi d = c$. Thus, 3.14 x 8 = 25.12 feet. Convert this to inches by multiplying by 12, which comes to 301.44". We know that we need a rise of 10.5", so we divide this number by 301.44, giving us .0348, or about 3.5 percent, which will be the grade required to elevate the track. A 3.5 percent grade is a little steep, but it is workable with small equipment. We now know that our basic design will work.

The next step requires transferring this information from paper to the railroad site. I like to mark the future roadbed directly on the ground with marking paint. Special cans of spray paint that are designed to be used upside down are available where landscape materials are sold.

The next step is to set the grade. To do this, you will need some wooden stakes about 24" long, some marker

Perspective and vanishing points

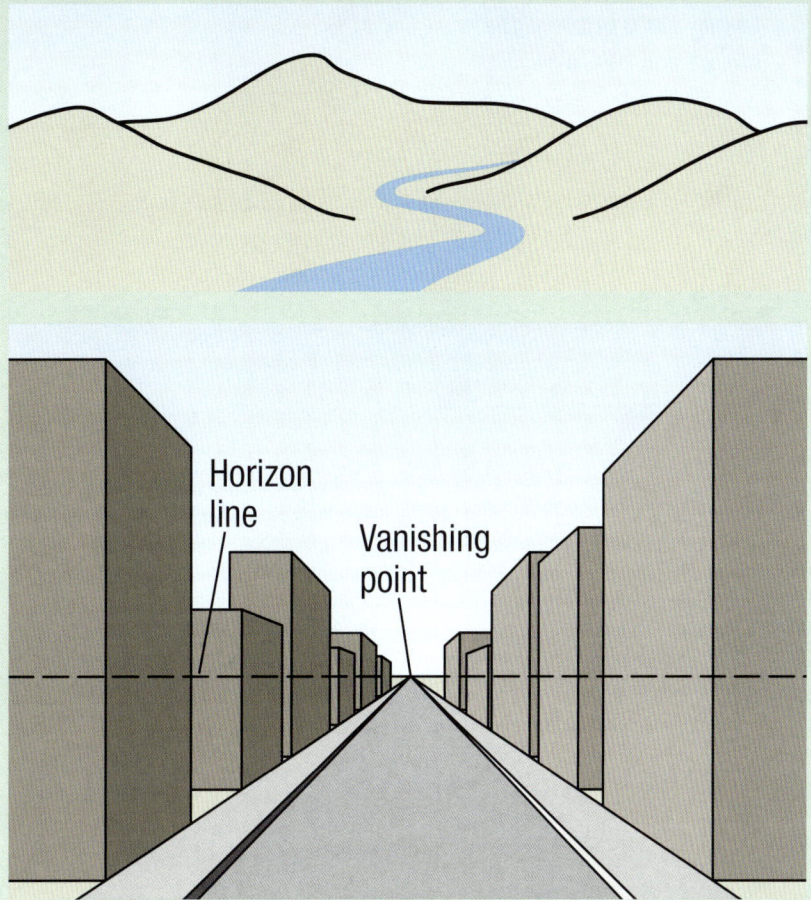

Horizon line

Vanishing point

It is beyond the scope of this book to go into a detailed explanation of vanishing points and perspective. Basic art books are available that explain these principles in detail. Here is an abridged version.

As things are seen by the eye, they appear smaller in the distance and larger up close. In looking at a set of parallel lines, such as a railroad track, the rails seem to meet at some point in the distance even though they are parallel. The point where they appear to meet is called the vanishing point.

In creating a garden-railroad scene, we can use this concept to create the illusion of greater space and depth. The easiest way to do this is to taper features that would normally have parallel lines, such as streets or roadways. Instead of making their sides parallel, draw them toward one another as they recede into the distance. Curving a road, for example, will enhance the effect.

This is most effective when you are working with an area that will usually be seen from a single spot. This is called "forced perspective." You are creating the illusion of distance by changing the parallel lines into converging ones. The same principle can be used with waterways and dry washes.

Another trick in forcing perspective is to make background items smaller, such as using smaller rocks at the top of the mountain instead of at the base. If you are using flat rocks, place the smaller end toward the vanishing point.

Using smaller-scale buildings can also force perspective. For example, if you use 1:22.5 buildings in the foreground, try using a 1:24 or 1:32-scale building in the background. If the building is far away, you might even be able to use a 1:48 (O scale) structure.

Try experimenting with this concept. You'll be amazed and pleased with some of the effects you can create.

Laying out a grade with stakes and PVC pipe

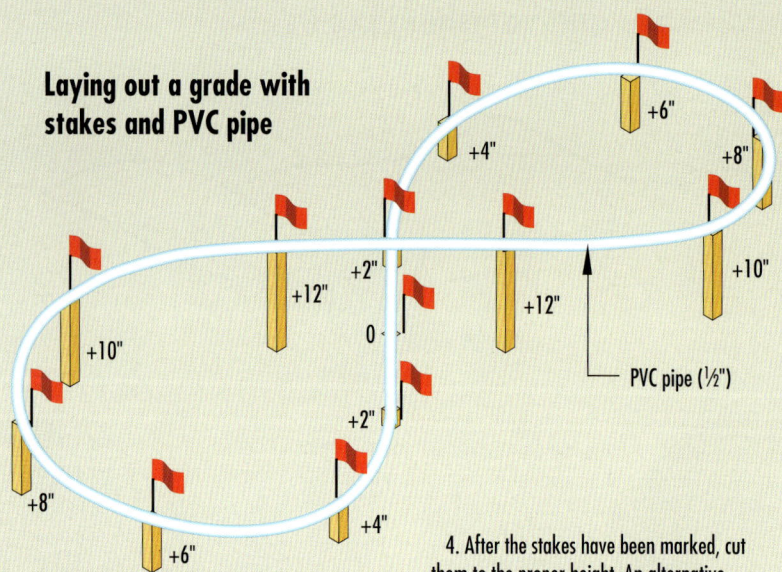

+6"

+4"

+8"

+12"

+2"

+10"

0

+12"

+10"

PVC pipe (½")

+2"

+8"

+4"

+6"

1. You can either use marker paint to lay out the track plan on the ground or start by laying out PVC pipe in the pattern of the proposed track plan, in this case a figure-eight.

2. Starting at the lowest point, drive a stake into the ground far enough that it is firmly planted. Measure 60" along the route and drive in the next stake. Repeat this every 60". Don't worry if the last stake is not 60" from the first.

3. Starting at the ground-level stake (0"), and using a transit or carpenter's level, mark the next stake at a point 2" higher than the first. Continue to the summit, marking each stake 2" higher than the last. When you reach the summit, reverse the process until you arrive back at ground level.

4. After the stakes have been marked, cut them to the proper height. An alternative method is to hammer them down to the correct level. If a stake is too low, attach another piece of wood cut to the proper height. The tops of the stakes will now serve as benchmarks.

Except in areas that suffer from frost heave, these stakes can stay in the ground forever, unless they need to be removed to make way for a bridge or trestle. They indicate the path of the railroad and the grade it will follow. The stakes would have to be closely followed on the small example shown here. On a larger line, the track could move to either side of the stakes without problems.

5. Next, attach the PVC pipe to the stakes. The author uses self-starting screws to do this. Screws can be removed as needed to temporarily remove the pipe.

is laid. Building the subroadbed first is what real railroads do, and there is a certain enjoyment in doing the same thing in your garden by first laying out a grade and then laying the track.

Design tips

It is best to work with a simple mainline track plan and use landscaping to create drama and interest. Add sidings after the mainline plan is established in your mind or on paper.

If you are using track power, avoid reverse loops in your design. These require special wiring and can be limiting in operation.

Avoid tight curves wherever possible. Curves cause drag on the train, and tighter curves create more drag. Broader curves result in smoother, more realistic, reliable operation. If you plan to run long trains, it is critical to have broad curves for proper operation. A full, sweeping curve adds a lot to the beauty of a railroad. Use as much room as you have to make a turn. If you have to tighten a curve, do it in the middle.

Consider elevating the railroad to provide better visibility and give you less distance to bend over. As little as six to 10 inches makes a big difference.

Consider multi-layered operation, where the trains run on two levels, as with a figure-eight, giving the railroad more depth.

Keep grades to 2 percent if possible. Most LGB engines can handle 3.5 percent grades with short trains. Anything steeper may require some weighting of the engines and could cause premature wear on gears and motors. If you have severe grades, plan to double-head your trains.

Use tunnels and rock formations to hide some of the turns and give the illusion that the train is going somewhere or has changed direction. In our figure-eight example, we are not trying to show that the track is laid in a figure-eight, but rather that the train changes direction and goes under itself. We want to see the sweeping curves and the bridge crossing over the main line. In general, real trains do not go in full circles. By hiding the entire loop from view, we can focus on a smaller part of the curve, making it seem larger than it really is.

flags, marker paint, and a transit or string level. You can also use a carpenter's level that has been rigged with an extension on the bottom of one end so that it reads level at 3.5 percent. To lay out the 3.5 percent grade, drive stakes into the ground along the proposed route, spaced 60" apart. (Any grade can be plotted this way by calculating the rise over 60". I use 60" because I find it handy to work with, but any number could be used.) Drive the stakes into the ground until they are firmly planted, with at least 12" sticking up. A 3.5 percent grade will rise 2.1" in a 60" run (2" is close enough for us to work with). Start at the ground-level stake and, working between it and the second stake with a transit or level, make a

mark 2" up on the second stake. Repeat the process at the following stakes until you reach the summit, then work your way back down to ground level.

Carefully cut off each stake at the mark. Paint the tops with bright marking paint and set a marker flag next to it. These are your grade stakes. (Note: If you live in an area affected by frost heaves, remove the stakes as the line is built. Otherwise, the stakes may be pushed up by frost, forcing your track out of alignment.)

If you were to fill the area up to the tops of the stakes, leaving a passage under the crossing, you could lay track and start running. However, I don't recommend this. It is difficult to work on the surrounding area once the track

2

Start working

The train has just emerged from a 15-foot-long tunnel cut into the hillside. The track is supported by a Swiss-style retaining wall. The rockwork and landscaping were built to form a mountain for the train to circumnavigate. *Photo by Marc Horovitz*

Many would-be great garden railroads suffer, both figuratively and literally, from the fatal error of flatness. This chapter shows you how to integrate your railroad into the existing landscape—even into a small space that might seem impossible to use—while keeping the railroad interesting and dynamic.

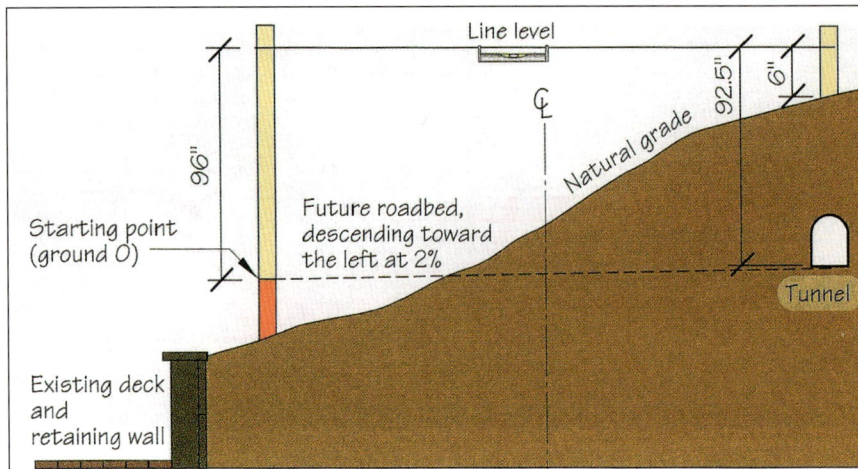

Fig. 1 – Section of existing terrain

To determine the depth of a tunnel in a hill, use a string level or transit, as explained in the last chapter. To do this on a steep slope, set up a string line over the area. Measure from the line down to the starting point (ground zero). The curve in our example has a 5-foot radius. By using the formula c = πd/2, we know the distance between the two points will be 188". Thus with a 2 percent grade, the tunnel floor should be approximately 3.5" higher than the starting point. From the grade calculations, we can determine that a trench 86" deep must be excavated for the tunnel.

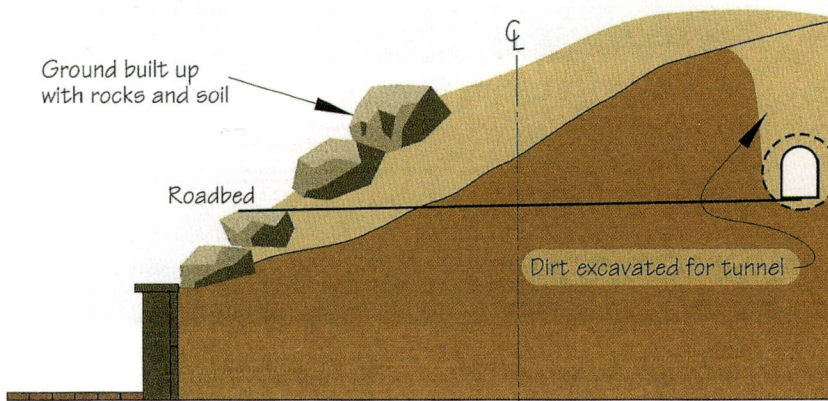

Labels in figures: Line level; 92.5"; 6"; CL; Natural grade; Starting point (ground 0); Future roadbed, descending toward the left at 2%; 96"; Tunnel; Existing deck and retaining wall; Ground built up with rocks and soil; Roadbed; CL; Dirt excavated for tunnel; Section as built

SECTION 1:
Hillside construction

I believe you can put a garden railroad into any available space, no matter how small it is or how awkwardly the land is laid out. I've built an operating garden railroad with living plants in a 16 x 24-inch space using a Z scale train. Another solution is to use a point-to-point system that does not require a turnaround. This could include a streetcar line or an industrial railroad.

An example of a challenging space is a hillside railroad that I built for Ed and Dorothy Barr. Both Ed and Dorothy are train enthusiasts, but they have different areas of interest. Ed likes the real Pennsylvania Railroad and is interested in switching operations. Dorothy is a fan of Swiss railroading and just enjoys watching the trains run. The decision was made to build two separate railroads, one for Ed and one for Dorothy.

The Barrs' house is on a steep slope, and there was no access to the railroad area for machinery or even a wheelbarrow. All materials had to be brought in by hand, up 14 steps. Eighty yards of soil and 12 tons of rock were carried in using black plastic buckets. The job looked impossible at first, but where there's a will, there's a way.

Dorothy wanted to run relatively long trains—five or six RhB passenger cars—on her Swiss railroad. The only suitable area for the line was on their very steep hillside. Fortunately, there was plenty of distance for a long run. The survey revealed that the area we had to work with was well over 50 feet long, about 11 feet wide at the narrow end, and wider at the other end, which would be out of sight for normal viewing.

The grade on the hillside was over 50 percent, so it was obvious that the trains weren't going that route. After studying the area, we decided that the track could run the 50-foot length and turn at each end, forming a large dogbone loop. This is the most basic of track plans, but the visual interest comes from the landscape and what happens along the route.

The main challenge was to provide a place for the train to turn around at the narrow end. After mentally analyzing a cross-section of the hillside, a solution appeared. By using the combination of a tunnel and bridge, we could provide a turnaround. We decided that instead of making a long, curved bridge, we would build a large mountain and make the train hug the edge of it, as railroads do in Switzerland.

Using the grade-stake method discussed in chapter 1, we laid out the turnaround. In this case, some stakes poked out of the ground while others hid below the survey line. After the mountain was built, we indicated the tunnel's path with marking paint and dug it out. Once the tunnel area was dug, the grade stakes were installed. In a deep tunnel like this, flexible drain pipe makes the best liner. The pipe was placed in the trench, with the bottom resting on the grade markers. The trench was then backfilled. We set grade markers 1" lower than the grade to compensate for the thickness of the pipe wall.

A string-level system or transit can be used to determine how deep a tunnel must be. To do this, set up a string line over the area. Measure from the line down to the starting point. In this example (**fig. 1**) it was at 96". We want the track to descend from the tunnel to the first grade stake (ground zero) on 2 percent grade. The turnaround track is a

2

five-foot radius. Using the formula for the circumference of a semicircle (c = πd/2), we find the distance between the two points is 188". With a 2 percent grade, the tunnel floor should be about 3.5" higher than the starting point. This is a case where a template is quite helpful.

Since relatively heavy trains would be running on this railroad, we wanted to limit the grade as much as possible, but still create the feeling of mountains. The "back" part of the line—the stretch of track farthest from the normal viewing area—was built relatively straight and at a slightly higher level than the front of the railroad. The real elevation changes were made in the curve as the train traverses the 2 percent grade through the long tunnel and around the mountain. Visual grade, or the illusion of a grade, is created by having the front track follow a more winding path, which makes the rear track appear higher and farther away than it really is. The entire line is actually relatively level, while the scenery rises above and falls below the level of the track.

The front line has an S-turn and passes through some short tunnels. In some areas, the ground was cut away below the track level, forming ravines, across which bridges were built. By varying the terrain, an illusion is created that the train is climbing or descending steep mountain grades. The feeling is further enhanced because the entire railroad is almost at eye level when seen from the main viewing area (**fig. 2**).

The back part of the line was built as far into the hillside as possible by using cuts and tunnels as necessary. A large portion of the front line was built up on bridges and viaducts, since this was the low side. In some areas, the soil and rock was mounded up as fill under the track so there wouldn't be too many viaducts and bridges.

▶ A pathway resembling a dry riverbed passes beneath a large stone arch bridge at the wide end of Dorothy Barr's railroad. Trackwork to the left, not seen in the photo, is hidden by shrubbery and supported on wooden benchwork. The end of the retaining wall is evident in the bottom right corner.
Photo by Marc Horovitz

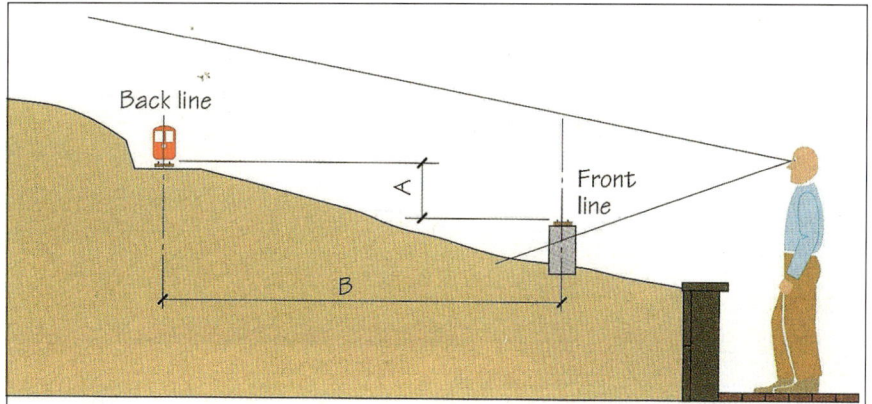

Fig. 2 – Eye-level viewing
The line at the rear is built as far back in the hillside as possible. "A" is the actual elevation separation between the front and back lines. By varying the distance "B," causing the train on the front line to be alternately closer to and farther from the viewer, the grade and altitude of the back line will appear to change more than it really does. To further emphasize this, the foreground can be built up or dug out, gaps can be spanned by bridges, and smaller hills and valleys can be built to make the lines appear to be separated by great distances.

At the broader (east) end, the hill dropped away into an open area. The roadbed at this point was about three feet up in the air. On the front track, the transition from the hillside to the open area was through a tunnel cut into the side of the mountain, then out onto a four-foot-long, three-foot-tall stone arch bridge (see the track plan below).

As the line heads out of sight into the bushes, the track is built on elevated wooden benchwork. This section can't be seen from the main viewing area, so it's not fancy. The benchwork was made of pressure-treated 4 x 4 fence posts set vertically into the ground with 2 x 4 cross members, then 2 x 12 boards laid between the posts to form a bed for the track (**fig 3**).

A socket-type fence-post anchor was driven into the ground first. The post was then dropped into the socket. The post could also have been set in cement or backfilled with sand and gravel. There are two schools of thought on this. Some think that a post set in concrete will rot off at the concrete line because water can't drain away, and that using sand or gravel remedies this. Others contend that by using pressure-treated wood, this problem is solved, at least for 40 years, which is what pressure-treated wood is rated for. The choice is yours.

◀ This small stone-arch bridge crosses a draw on the front line. It adds to the beauty of the scene and creates a sense of balance. *Photo by Marc Horovitz*

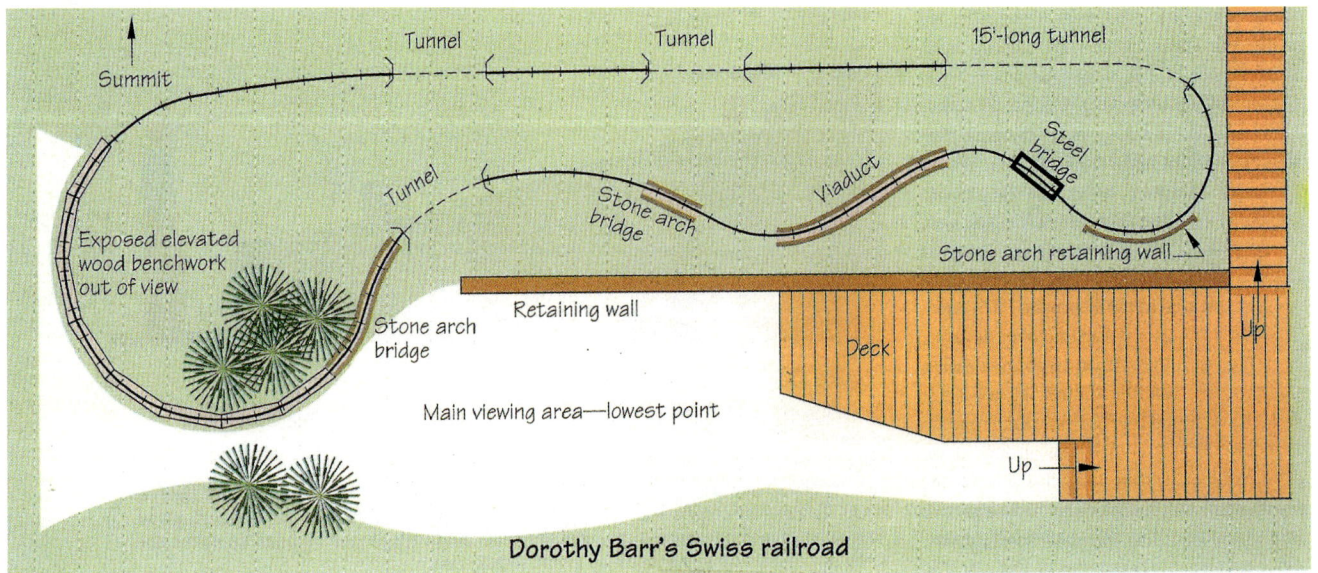

Dorothy Barr's Swiss railroad

Elevated track

Track built on elevated, pressure-treated benchwork is a simple solution for areas that are hidden from view. Posts (4 x 4s) are used for the uprights, while 2 x 4s form the cross pieces. The track base is made from 2 x 12s on curves and 2 x 6s on straight sections. First, set the posts. Mark the post at a grade elevation minus the thickness of the track base and trim it to height. Attach the 2 x 4 cross pieces to the posts with deck screws. Screw the track base to the 2 x 4s and posts for extra strength. Curved sections can be cut with a saber saw to match the track curvature, if you wish. In our example, the track is ballasted, and the ballast is used for minor height adjustments. Redwood bender board edging holds the ballast in place.

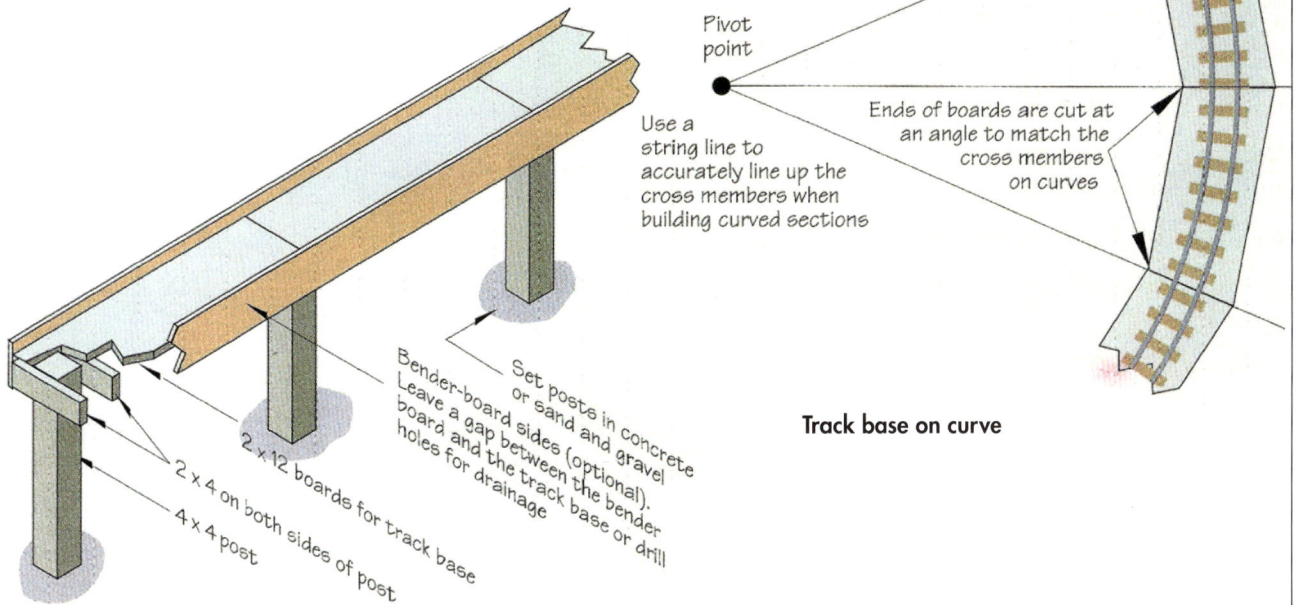

String line

Pivot point

Use a string line to accurately line up the cross members when building curved sections

Ends of boards are cut at an angle to match the cross members on curves

Set posts in concrete or sand and gravel

Bender-board sides (optional). Leave a gap between the bender board and the track base or drill holes for drainage

2 x 12 boards for track base

2 x 4 on both sides of post

4 x 4 post

Track base on curve

Fig. 3 – Elevated track base

The train winds its way along an S-curve on the front line. This curve pulls the front line away from the rear line and gives the scene more depth. *Photo by Marc Horovitz*

SECTION 2:
Creating a three-dimensional railroad on a flat site

Working with a flat area can be as challenging as dealing with a grade. The problem is how to take an uninteresting space and create a landscape that has both depth and interest.

The figure-eight is a versatile design that can create great depth. In fact,

when working with a small area, this may be the only practical track plan to create depth. In a larger area, however, a single figure-eight may look a little spartan. Even though I prefer less track than more, there still needs to be enough of a main line to keep things interesting. I have used similar track plans, all variations of the folded dogbone, on several railroads that were built on flat ground.

The folded dogbone in **fig. 4** offers a lot of landscaping possibilities. The track passes over and under itself at two or more places, which helps achieve the

▲ Kent Kirkorian's railroad features a folded-dogbone design, and the layered effect is apparent. The train is on an ascending track. Its next stop will be the high-level yard at the back of the railroad (not shown). Once it leaves this yard, it will go around the mountain in the background and descend over the trackage to the right of the train, traveling through a tunnel and ending up in the low-level yard. *Photo by Marc Horovitz*

three-dimensional or layered look when viewed from scale eye level. There can be two large turning loops at each end, since the loops overlap. For example, in a 12-foot-wide space, you could have two overlapping turning loops that are each 10 feet in diameter (**fig. 5**). A train will travel from right to left twice and from left to right twice, each time on a different track, which adds interest to the line.

The folded dogbone is a simple plan, and the main line flows nicely. Through the creative use of landscaping and a few track plan variations, you can keep guests wondering where the train is going next or exactly where it is when it goes out of sight. To add more interest to this basic design, a series of sidings and towns can be incorporated to give the railroad purpose (**fig. 6**). Space permitting, a smaller, separate point-to-point mining, logging, or industrial railroad could be incorporated into the line as well.

A minimum of two tunnels and two bridges are usually required to make this design work visually, though you could add many more. The simplified track plan shows only the basic concept. The actual roadbed can be moved in a variety of ways to create interest, and the railroad can be elevated above grade in several places if you wish to incorporate trestles and bridges.

Another track plan that allows the railroad to climb over itself to create interest is a simple loop or dogbone that includes a climbing loop at each end of the line (**fig. 7**). This plan may be better suited for an area that is too narrow to encompass the four lines of the folded-dogbone plan. Towns and villages can be built within or around these loops.

Remember, the basic philosophy is to take a simple track plan and add to existing grades or make them look steeper. An optical illusion can be created if the landscape rock and terrain are made to descend as the track ascends. This causes the eye to see a steeper grade than actually exists.

Design hints for working with flat ground

If at all possible, raise the entire area in which the railway is contained. Build the lowest rail line 12" to 18" higher

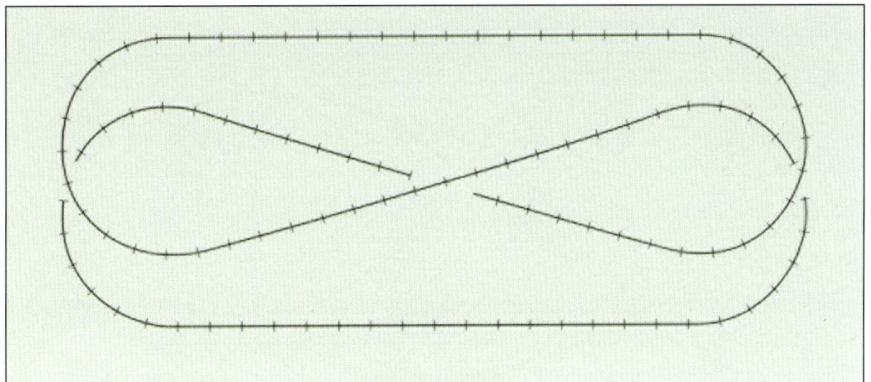

Fig. 4 – The folded dogbone track plan
The folded dogbone is a deceptively simple track plan. The track passes over and under itself several times in a complete circuit of the line, presenting many landscaping opportunities.

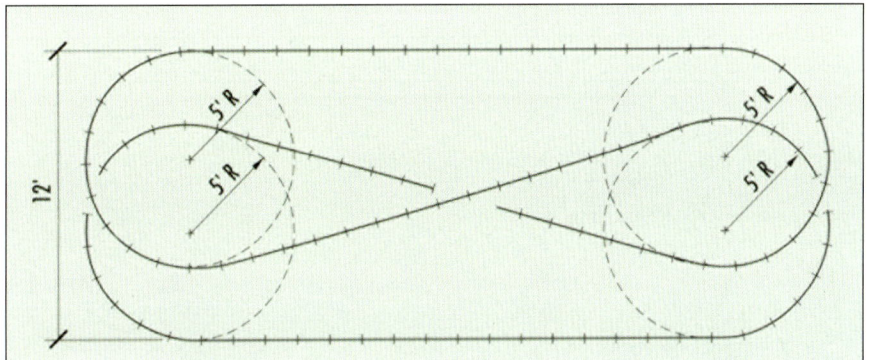

Fig. 5 – A space saver
The folded dogbone is also a space saver. You can have two relatively large turning loops at each end in just a little more space than it would take for one loop. For example, you could have two five-foot-radius turns in a space as little as 12 feet wide. Bear in mind, it takes a space 10 feet wide to have one five-foot-radius turning loop.

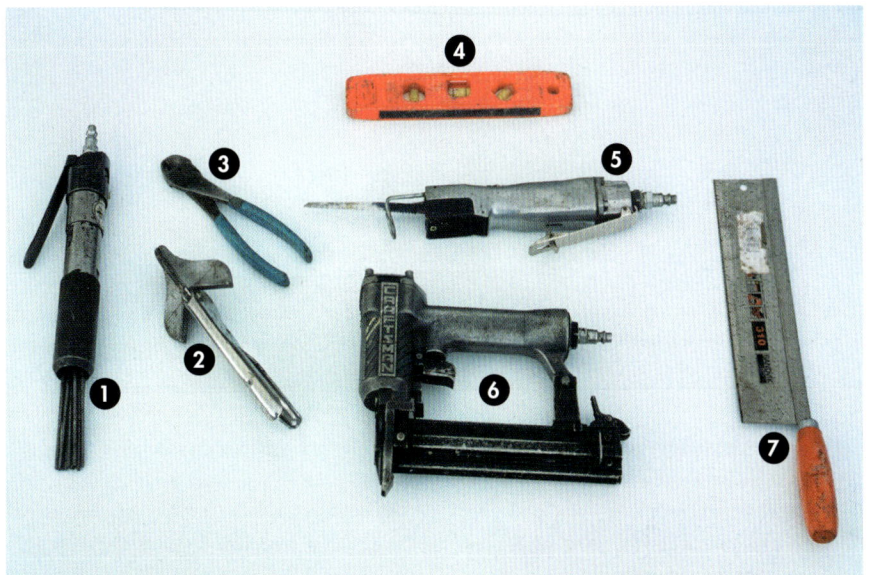

These are the basic tools for trestle building and assembly: 1. Needle gun or scaler. 2. Wood-cutting tool. 3. Side cutters. 4. Torpedo level. 5. Air saw. 6. Brad gun. 7. Dovetail saw. Several of these tools are air-powered; electric tools work as well.

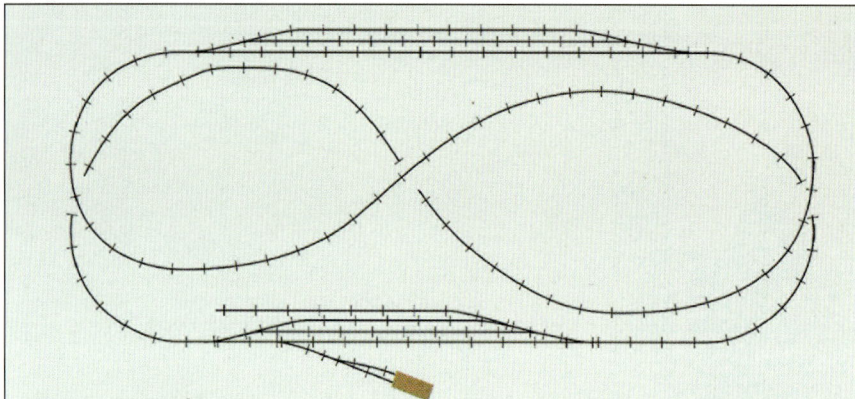

Fig. 6 – Versatility
In actual practice, you may wish to vary the route to suit your taste and imagination, while still maintaining the basic plan. A series of passing sidings and/or spurs can be added to the line to make prototypical operation possible. If space permits, a small point-to-point railroad can also be added.

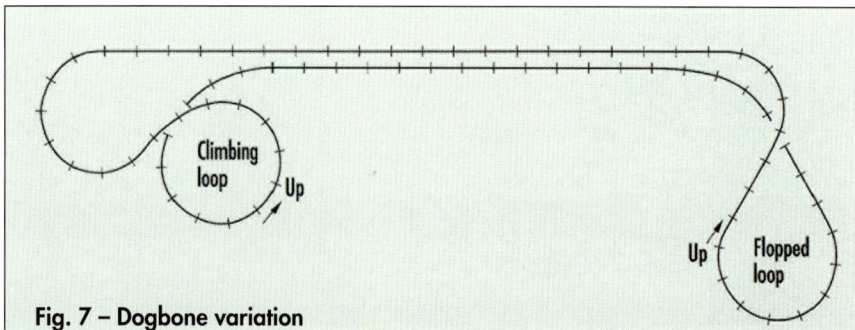

Fig. 7 – Dogbone variation
One possible variation is an unfolded dogbone with one end flopped to form a crossing (right), and a climbing loop similar to Colorado's Georgetown Loop added to the other end. These could be reversed, or you could have the same type of loop at both ends. The main idea is to incorporate changes in elevation into the railroad. In this plan, only two apparent lines travel east and west, as opposed to four apparent lines in the folded dogbone. This plan could be used in an area where there is room at the ends but limited space in the middle, such as a flower bed.

than the pathway or ground level. Use the stake-grade method discussed earlier to lay out your track plan as well as the grade.

If you would like a relatively flat track for live-steam operation, a way to obtain the illusion that the train is changing elevations is, again, to raise the entire line off the ground. In this case, however, the result is not an over-and-under track plan, but rather a simple loop. The next step would be to vary the landscaping around the line. Mountains can climb above the level of the track, and valleys would fall below, while the train stays on a constant, level grade.

Plan your railroad so that from the normal viewing point the terrain in the background is at the highest point and the foreground is at the lowest (**fig. 8**). The area in between can vary. This will give the illusion of greater distance. If the entire railroad is elevated, some of the landscaping can actually be below track level, for example a dry wash or canyon. If you are building at grade (in other words, at ground level—not elevated above the natural grade of the land), you will have to provide drainage where the landscape goes below grade, or you may end up with a lake.

Consider building towns or villages in a place where some of the landscape is higher than the town and some is lower. This will frame the scene, providing a backdrop for the town and making it look like it is set in the mountains.

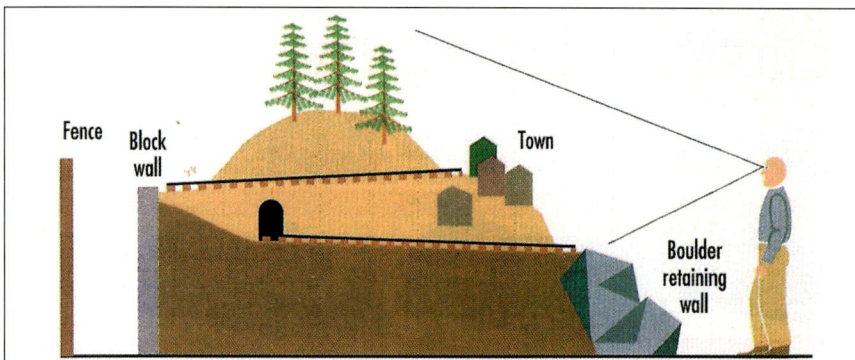

Fig. 8 – Elevating the line
The track in the foreground should be at the lowest point on the railway, and the track at the back should be at the highest. This allows the viewer to see more of the railroad. Scenery that varies in height adds to the realism of the scene.

Different methods can be used to raise the railroad. If you want a natural look, use boulders to form a retaining wall in the foreground, then blend in the landscaping. If you want a more formal setting, you can use bricks or concrete blocks to make a retaining wall. This will provide a sharp rise and actually give you more railroad real estate, since the wall does not angle back as boulders used as retainers would. Using a formal wall is like framing a picture.

Since the rear of the railroad is the highest point, it is almost always better to use a formal retaining wall to make a sharp rise. This is especially true if you are working in a confined space where the back of the line may be against a fence.

Note: if you are building a retaining wall along a fence line, be sure to leave enough space to install a new fence when the time comes. It is a good idea to replace an old fence before building your railroad.

Climbing loops & switchbacks

Another way to deal with a sloping site, especially a steep one, is by using switchbacks and climbing loops.

An interesting problem was presented to me by David McGuinness and his son Nicholas. Dave's home sits on the old Sacramento Northern Railroad right-of-way. In fact, part of a tunnel portal is still visible in his backyard. Some years ago, the cut leading to the tunnel was filled in to form the lot for the house. Dave's yard has a severe slope. It's not quite a cliff, but it's not far from it. He wanted me to design and install a logging railroad that would climb his hill. The available area was about 50 feet wide by 50 feet deep, but not all was usable for the railroad.

Dave's site had a hidden asset. A few years back, a city water main broke. Water flowing down his hillside enlarged an existing crevice. This crevice was later used to create a stream and waterfalls for the railroad, as well as a large canyon.

Climbing the grade

Starting at the log pond at the bottom, the line travels north up a steady 3.5 percent grade, then enters an up-and-over climbing loop. The line then heads south, continuing upgrade while crossing the canyon on a trestle.

At the south end of the trestle, there was no room to turn. The track at this point is on a sheer cliff, so a switchback was used (**fig. 9**). As the train travels south, it heads into the tail of the switchback, where it stops while the switch is thrown to the alternate route. It then leaves the switchback in reverse, heading north. It crosses the canyon again to a mountain ridge, which it follows to the log landing at the upper end of the line, about six feet higher than the mill pond.

Along the route, trains cross the water four times. This railroad proves my theory that the more difficult the terrain seems, the better the railroad will look.

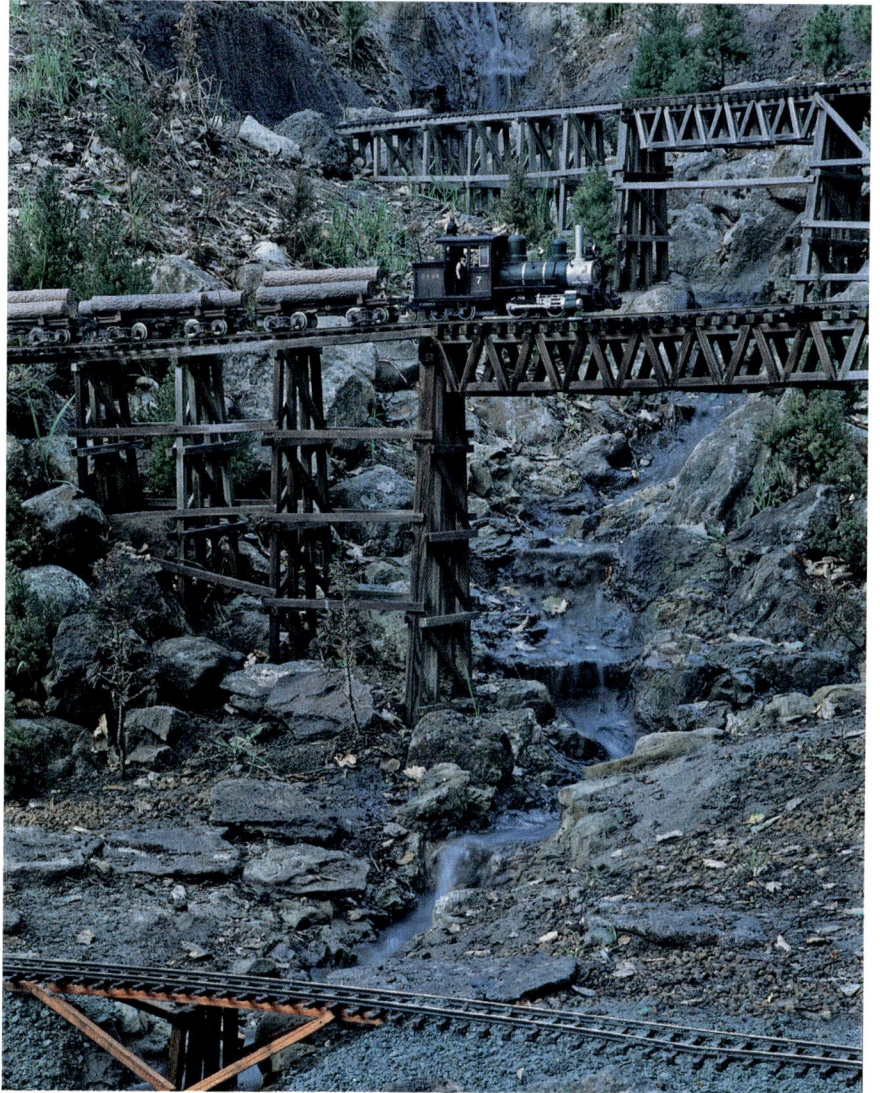
On Dave McGuinness's railroad, trains must climb six feet from the mill pond to the log landing, crossing five major trestles and bridges on the way.

A hillside railroad can offer fantastic views. A feeling of great depth and distance can be created by using height to force the perspective. The train is descending the high trestle.

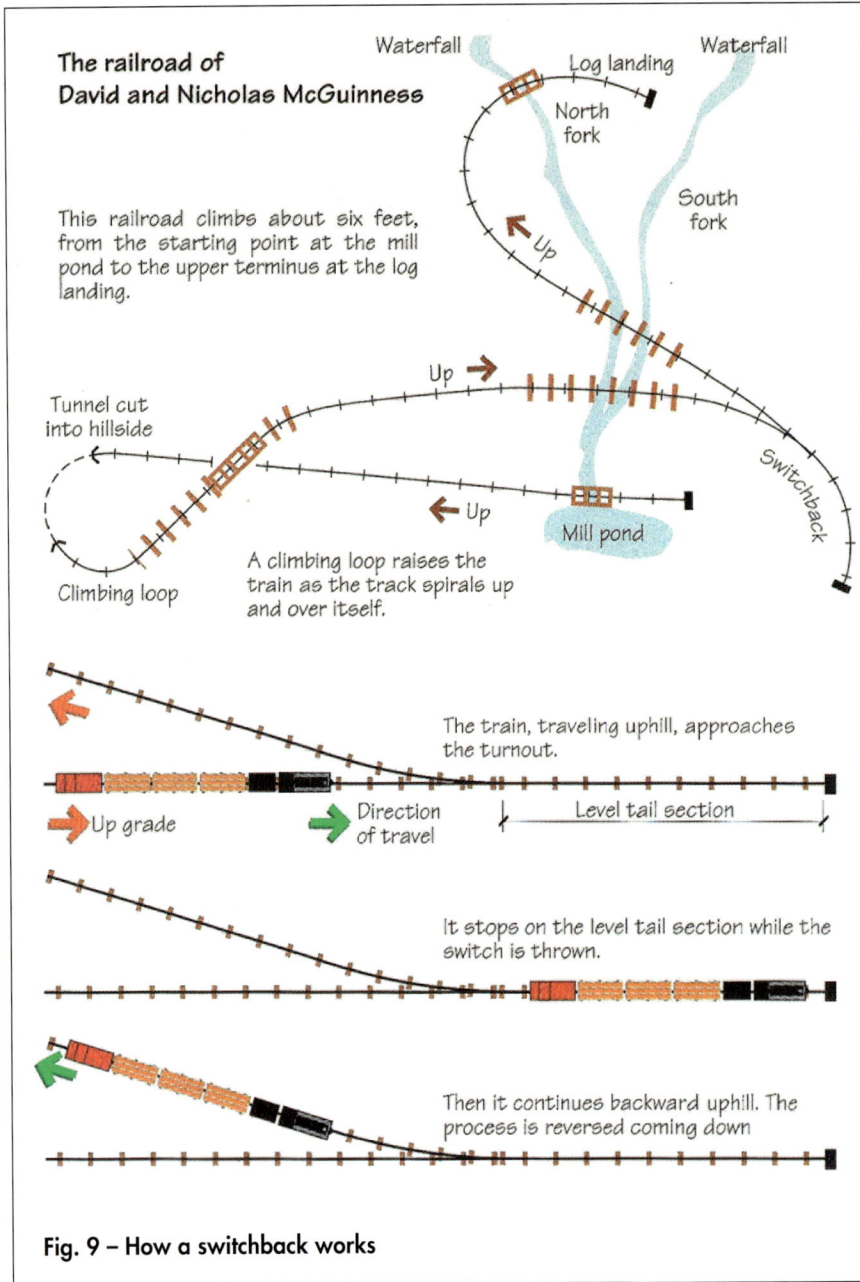

The railroad of David and Nicholas McGuinness

Waterfall   Log landing   Waterfall

North fork

South fork

This railroad climbs about six feet, from the starting point at the mill pond to the upper terminus at the log landing.

Up

Tunnel cut into hillside

Up →

Switchback

← Up

Climbing loop

Mill pond

A climbing loop raises the train as the track spirals up and over itself.

The train, traveling uphill, approaches the turnout.

→ Up grade   → Direction of travel   Level tail section

It stops on the level tail section while the switch is thrown.

Then it continues backward uphill. The process is reversed coming down

Fig. 9 – How a switchback works

Due to the size of the yard, the depth of the crevice, and the rise in elevation, the railroad can be viewed from many angles. The canyon provides a lot of depth. The general viewing area is at the base of the hill, which puts most of the railroad at eye level or higher. This adds to the illusion of greater distance.

Switchbacks

Railroads and road builders use different types of switchbacks. One employs a tail track that requires the train to go past a turnout, stop while the points are reset, then continue up the grade in reverse. If there is a lot of elevation to gain, this back-and-forth process can be repeated as many times as necessary with multiple switchbacks.

Another type of switchback is a horseshoe curve, on which the train turns as it ascends. A climbing loop is another way to gain elevation. Two famous examples of this are the Tehachapi Loop and the Georgetown Loop. In these, the track travels up and around, ultimately crossing over itself. With long trains, the engine can actually pass over the caboose.

Automatic switchbacks

If you favor the engineer operating theory discussed in the introduction, a switchback offers a lot of action. You must clear the switch and stop the train. Then you must reset the switch to the new route and reverse the train to enter the next leg of the switchback.

For the person who just likes to be an observer, this sounds like work! There is a solution for the observer types, though. A switchback can be fully automated using some LGB parts and an LGB no. 80090.

Components

Let's deal with the turnout first. The challenge is that the turnout must be thrown properly, depending on which way the train is running. To accomplish this, you will need the following LGB (or equivalent) parts:

Qty.	Part no.	Description
3	LGB 17000	Track contact
1	LGB 17010	Switching magnet
2	LGB 12010	EPL switch drive
1	LGB 12030	Supplementary switch unit
1		Bridge rectifier

The contact (no. 17000) is a reed switch that clips onto the track between two ties. When a locomotive or car equipped with a magnet passes over it, the switch is momentarily actuated.

The no. 17000 has three terminals (**fig. 10**). The center terminal is common, and the two outer ones are positive and negative. One leg of an AC power source is connected to the common terminal of the switch, while the other leg is connected to the device being controlled. A third wire goes from the controlled device to one of the remaining outputs of the no. 17000. Depending on which side is hooked up, a switch motor (for instance) can be thrown either right or left. If the two outer terminals on the no. 17000 are connected by a jumper, the device will function as a momentary on/off switch.

A magnet (no. 17010) is used to actuate the no. 17000 switch. This is fastened to the bottom of a locomotive or piece of rolling stock.

A switch motor (LGB no. 12010) is normally used to throw the points of a turnout, but it can also be fitted with a supplementary switch unit that will cause it to act as a relay.

The supplementary switch unit (LGB no. 12030) is a pair of single-pole, double-throw (SPDT) switches that can be connected to the no. 12010 switch motor. These can be used for a variety of functions, such as routing track power, controlling signals or lights, or, in our case, changing track polarity.

A bridge rectifier (available at Radio Shack or other electronics-supply stores) is a device that converts AC input to DC output. It's used here to convert AC to DC to activate the switchback's turnout.

How it all works

In the automatic turnout-control circuit, the components do the following jobs (**fig. 10**):

The locomotive is fitted with a no. 17010 magnet, which is attached to the bottom of its motor block. As it runs over the eastbound contact (No. 1), it sends a positive signal to the switch motor fitted with the supplementary switch unit (No. 3), which has been wired as a polarity-reversing switch. This signal resets the polarity of the power that will eventually throw the switch points (No. 5). At this point, nothing on the railroad has actually changed. Only the polarity that will determine which way the points will be thrown has been set. As the locomotive passes over the turnout-activator contact (No. 4, a no. 17000 that has been wired as a simple on/off switch), it throws the points to the new route.

The train now reverses onto the new route, where the engine passes over the westbound contact (No. 2) and a negative signal is sent to the polarity-reversing switch (No. 3) to set up the polarity change that will throw the points on the return trip.

At the very end of the line, the train stops and reverses direction. It will pass over the westbound contact (No. 2) again, but nothing will happen this time, since the change was made with the first pass. The train will then pass over the turnout-activator contact (No. 4) again, at which time the points will be reset so the train can head out the other way.

The train, coming from the upper section of the line, enters the tail track of the switchback. From there it will continue down the line in reverse.

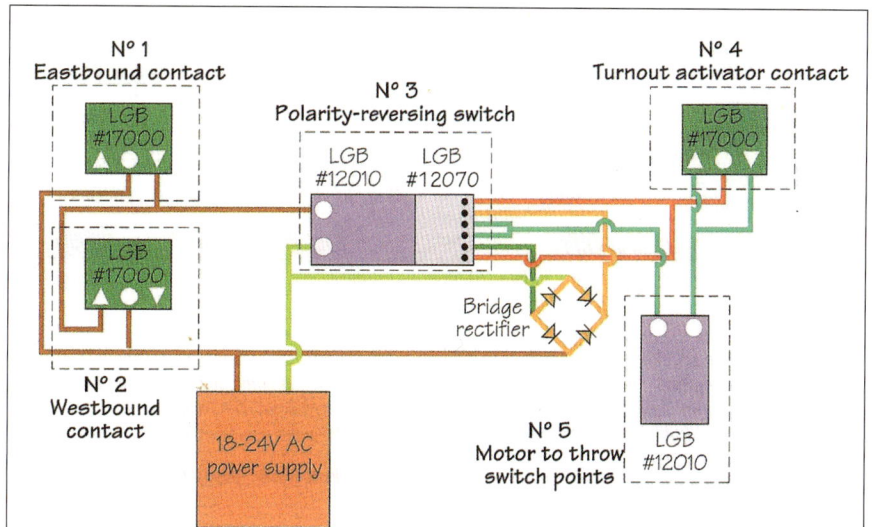

Component locations
1 & 2. Contacts are set about 12" from the turnout
3. Polarity-reversing switch can be mounted in any suitable location
4. Turnout-activator contact must be set far enough into the tail track that the last car of the train is clear of the points when they move
5. The motor to throw the points is mounted on the turnout

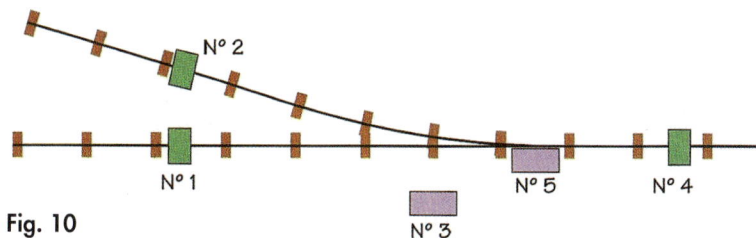

Fig. 10
Automatic turnout control for switchbacks

Connect one lead from the LGB #10340 to the common (unbroken) rail and one to the rail between the diodes

DC in | Max. time
Track out | Min. time

LGB #10340   Power supply

To make the gap, cut the rail, then reconnect it with an insulating rail clamp, leaving a small gap between the pieces. Insert a thin piece of 1/16"-wide plastic between the rails to keep them isolated.

A diode has a stripe at one end to indicate direction of current. If your engine runs off the end of the track, the diode has been installed backward and must be reversed.

Plastic insulating strip

Power rail clamp

Insulated rail clamp

Diode

Gapping the rail

The engine will stop as soon as it enters a gapped section. In a switchback, the train will always run in reverse over at least two legs. Set the gaps to allow for this. For example, if the train started on Leg A, the engine would enter Leg B first. The gap must be set so that the last car clears the switch before the train stops. On Legs A and C, the gap must be set so that the engine stops before the cars run off the end of the track. All engines coast a little so allow some extra clearance.

Leg C

Gap must always be in the same rail.

Gap

Leg A

Gap

Gap

Leg B

Note: Railroads that operate on steep grades, especially rack lines, often run with the locomotive on the down-grade side of the train to prevent runaway rolling stock, should the couplers fail. (On some lines, where the entire line is on a grade, the trains don't even have couplers; just push plates.) Running this way is also good practice on a garden line. If this is your choice, set your gaps accordingly.

Gap locations for automatic reversing units in switchbacks

Fig. 11

In simpler terms, contacts Nos. 1 and 2 in conjunction with polarity-reversing switch No. 3 just reset the polarity that will throw the switch points to the right or left. Switch No. 4 actually triggers the action. The system works automatically as the engine passes over the contacts. All you have to do is start and stop the train and reverse its direction at the appropriate times. The system will work with any locomotive equipped with a suitable magnet, including battery power or live steam.

If you are using track power and want your train to run automatically, with completely hands-off operation, it can be done with the addition of an automatic reversing unit such as the LGB no. 10340 (**fig. 11**). This device is basically a timer. One side is connected to the power supply's throttle control, and the other side is connected to the track (between gapped sections described later). The no. 10340 doesn't control the speed of the train, just the direction. The timing function can be adjusted. It can

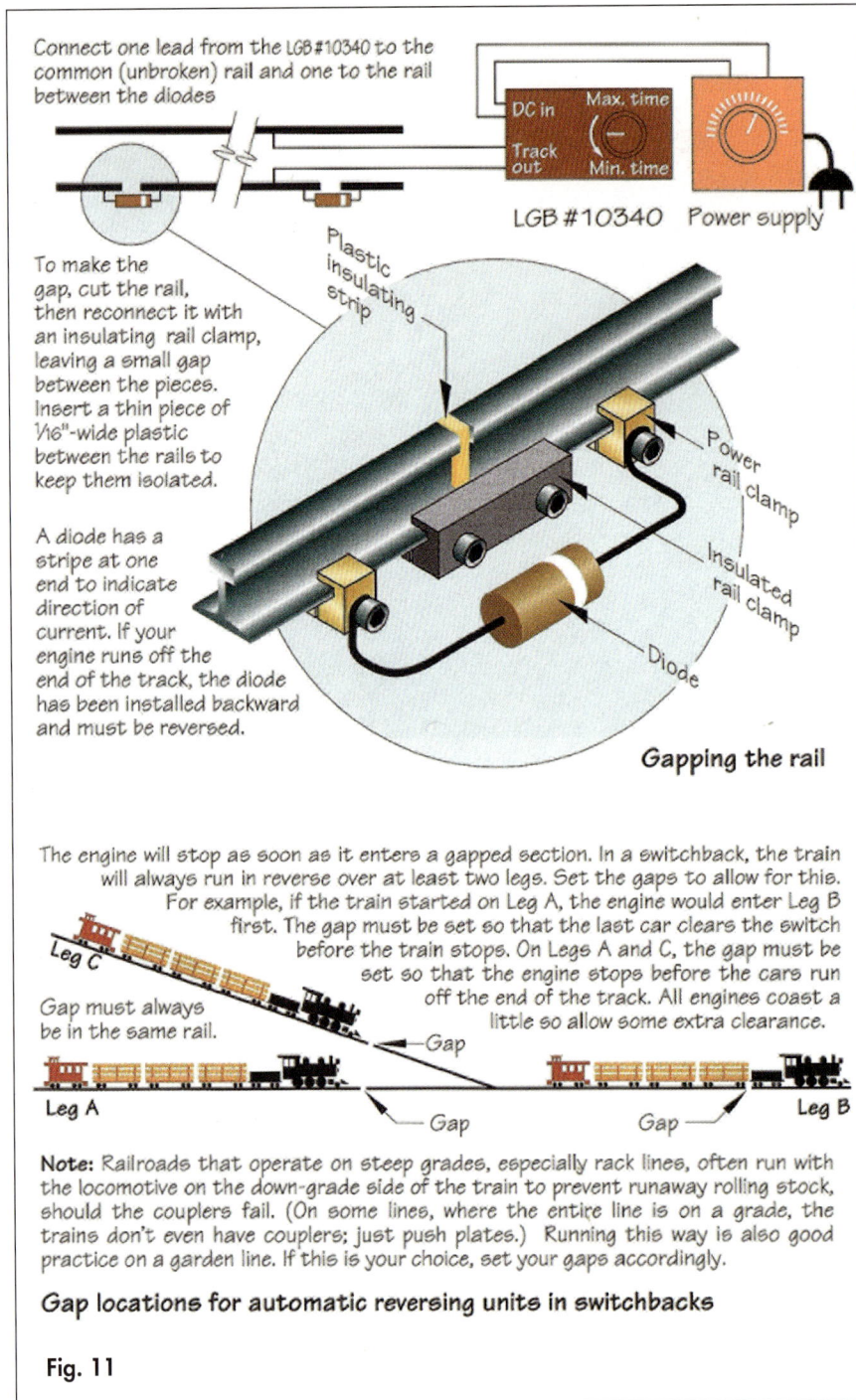

be set, for example, to run the train for 90 seconds in one direction, then 90 seconds in the other. The no. 10340 simply changes the polarity for 90 seconds at a time. In the meantime, the reverse is happening at the other end of the line in the opposite gapped section.

In other words, one end of the line is dead while the other is live. This changes when the polarity is reversed. In reality, the no. 10340 doesn't start and stop the train. This is done by the reaction of the diodes to the polarity change. As a safety measure, it's a good idea to add a gapped section at the end of any siding to prevent the locomotive from running off the end of the track.

Hooking it up

To add automatic control, begin by connecting the track to the track-power leads from the no. 10340 (**fig. 11**). Connect one lead to the common (unbroken) rail and the other to the gapped rail between the diodes. An easy way to insulate and connect the diodes is to use Railclamps from Richard Hillman or a similar product from another manufacturer. For each gap you will need:

Qty.	Part #	Description
1	332-01P	Plastic insulated rail clamp
2	332-015	Power clamp
1		1/16"-wide thin piece of plastic
2		Diodes*

*LGB supplies diodes that are built into sections of track, but I prefer to use diodes as shown here. Use diodes that are rated to handle at least 1 amp at 24 volts.

To make the insulated gap, cut the rail, then reconnect the two pieces with the plastic rail clamp. Be sure to leave a gap between the ends of the rails. Insert the 1/16"-wide plastic between the rails to keep them from touching.

Install the diodes by first connecting a power clamp to each side of the gap. Then connect the diode's leads to the power clamps by wrapping the lead around the screw or attaching it to a wire-end connector.

2

Once the switchback has been properly wired, the engine will stop as soon as it enters the gapped section. In a switchback, the train will always run in reverse on at least two legs of its journey. Set your gap to allow for this.

For example, in looking at **fig. 11**: If the train started out at point A, heading for point B with the engine pulling the cars behind it, the engine would enter Leg B first with the cars trailing. The gap must be set so the last car of the train clears the switch points before the train stops.

At points A and C, the gaps must be set so the engine comes to a stop before the cars run off the end of the track. All engines coast a little, so allow some extra clearance.

SECTION 4:
Horseshoe curves & painted backdrops

The site for Frank Swarb's line is set on a gradual hillside. If a train were to assault the hill head on, it would be climbing a 15 percent grade. This would not be impossible for a cog railroad, but Frank wanted to run standard steam engines on a single-track main line. The goal was to design a railroad that would handle engines like the LGB Mogul using grades no steeper than 3.5 percent. To solve the problem, horseshoe curves were employed.

▲ The train is rounding the upper loop, heading for tunnel No. 2. A horseshoe curve can be seen below it. Scenery above and below the train helps make the area look larger. Landscaping should dwarf the train.

Horseshoe curves are used to divide the climb. If you're a sailor, think of it as sailing to an up-wind destination. You can't sail directly into the wind, so you must tack back and forth to reach your goal. For a land man, it's like riding a one-speed bike uphill: You can crisscross the path to cut the climb into smaller, more manageable parts. This is what we do with the train. Instead of climbing the hill all at once, it can go up more easily by switching back and

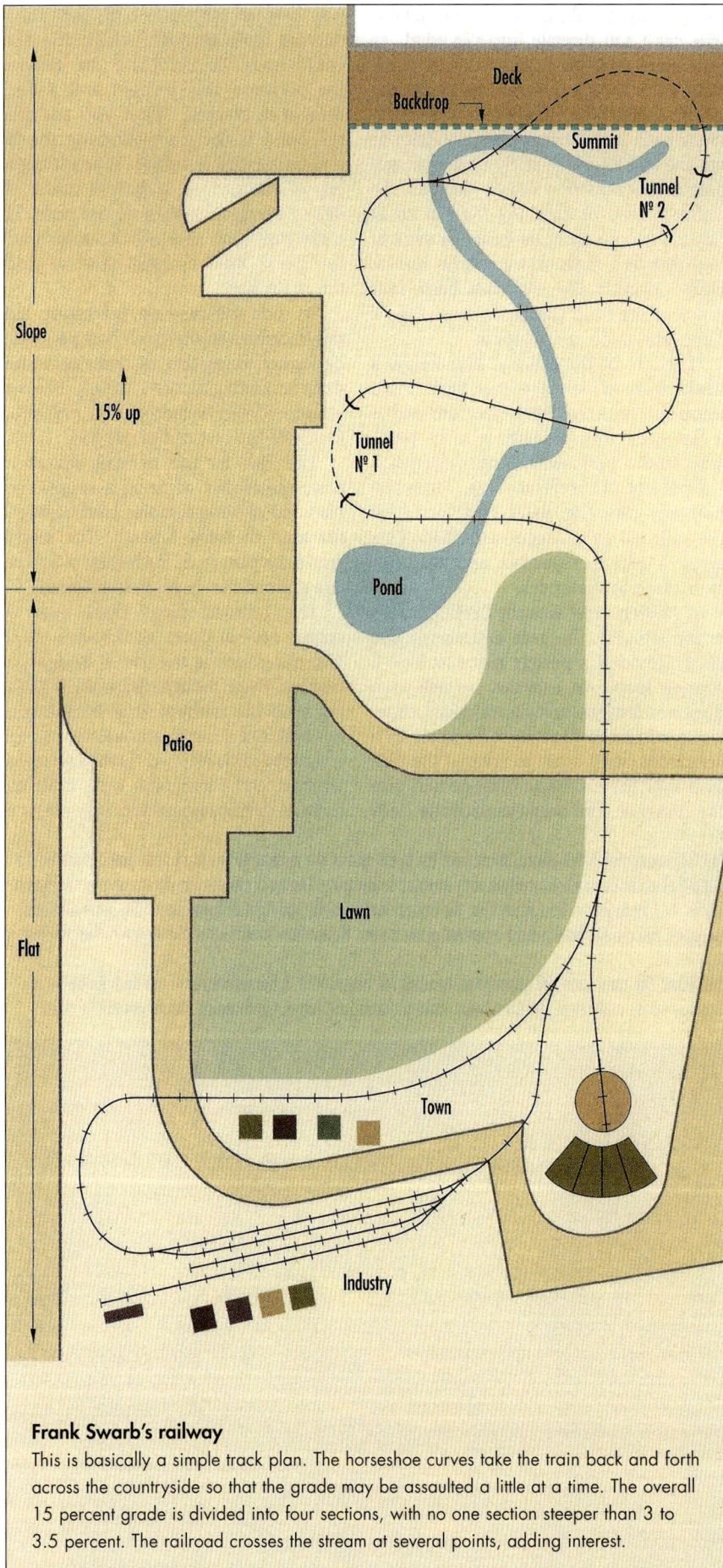

Frank Swarb's railway

This is basically a simple track plan. The horseshoe curves take the train back and forth across the countryside so that the grade may be assaulted a little at a time. The overall 15 percent grade is divided into four sections, with no one section steeper than 3 to 3.5 percent. The railroad crosses the stream at several points, adding interest.

forth on horseshoe curves. Frank's line switches back four times, which limits the grade to 3 percent at any point.

The site of the railroad is below a deck, from which you can look down at the railroad. At the bottom end is a flat area with a lawn, a brick pathway, and a patio with built-in benches—a perfect observation area. From the pathway and the patio, you can view the railroad as it ascends the hill. This gives a nice perspective and the illusion of great distance.

Exposed reverse loops don't always look prototypical, especially in relatively small areas, but an asset on Frank's line was the deck. Located at the summit, the area underneath the deck provided a perfect place to hide a reverse loop. To create the illusion that the train had disappeared into the distance, the area beneath the deck was covered with a Masonite hardboard backdrop, with a hole through which the line could pass. The Masonite was painted to complete the illusion. What viewers now see from the patio is the train climbing the hill and going into a tunnel. When it comes out of the tunnel, it passes under the deck through a hidden access hole. The train continues around the loop, under the deck, then emerges and re-enters the main line.

To hide the hole on the return side, the backdrop in this area was painted in dark-gray tones like distant mountains. The backdrop's foreground was painted to match the rest of the railroad.

The plan for this railroad follows my basic philosophy of using a simple track plan and creating complex landscaping for the train to travel through. The loop-to-loop track plan gives the feeling of a mountain railroad that is going somewhere.

The railroad crosses the stream several times as it winds up the hill, necessitating the use of bridges and trestles. Even though the train is climbing a hillside, without some help it would not look like a mountainous area. To help create this illusion, two tunnels were constructed and mountains were built over them. A scenic opportunity was presented each time the train crossed the water, and several types of bridges were used. A switch yard was installed on the flat area

around the lawn. The reverse loop at this end is much larger than the one at the summit, so it was not necessary to hide it. The loop is actually part of the rail yard, so it is not so obvious that the track forms a loop. On paper, the track plan looks simple, but when the scenery is added, it comes to life.

Backdrops

If you are lucky enough to have a pleasant, natural background for your railroad, then backdrops may not be of interest to you. Sometimes, though, there are things behind your railroad that are not visually pleasing—an old fence, a neighbor's unkempt house, or, in this case, the underbelly of a deck.

My first choice is always to use an existing natural backdrop, such as a hedge, or try to create one. In some cases, though, it is difficult to control what's in the background. A painted backdrop can help solve these problems by hiding unsightly objects while creating an illusion of space at the same

time. A simple backdrop can be made of exterior-grade Masonite hardboard or synthetic signboard material fastened to the fence or, in our case, mounted under the deck. This is then painted to create a pleasing background.

Tips on painting backdrops

Use non-rusting fasteners to attach the backdrop to its support. Brass or stainless-steel screws will prevent rust streaks from appearing on your "sky."

You do not have to be an artist to paint a backdrop. A backdrop should be just that: a backdrop, not a mural. You don't want it to stand out or draw attention to itself, so don't include a lot of detail. Simple rolling hills and some trees are all that is necessary.

If you are using Masonite, paint all sides and edges first with primer. Then paint the entire backdrop a very light blue. I want to emphasize *light* blue—it's easy to overdo it. A natural sky is lightest at the horizon, becoming darker at higher elevations. This can be

▲ The train traverses a through truss bridge that hides a septic-tank cover. The pony truss bridge in the foreground provides another one of the stream crossings. In the background is the unobtrusive painted backdrop that hides the deck's underside.

achieved by tinting your basic light blue paint a little darker as you go up the board. This detail is more for photography than for general viewing, so you don't have to do this if you want to keep it simple.

You could paint a backdrop with the sky color only. However, if you want to blend the backdrop into the scenery, you can do so by painting low mountains or hills that look like a continuation of the actual scenery. Keep these painted mountains and hills low! Usually 3" to 4" of height is all that's required for the effect. Keep in mind that the backdrop must not dominate the scene.

Distant mountains look purple or violet and show little detail. Closer hills and mountains can be brown or green,

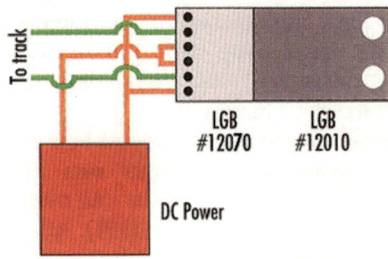

This is how LGB's book shows to hook up the polarity-reversing circuit for a reverse loop using their components. It works, but can cause a momentary short circuit when actuated. This may not be a problem with most power packs, but could cause a more sensitive system to shut down.

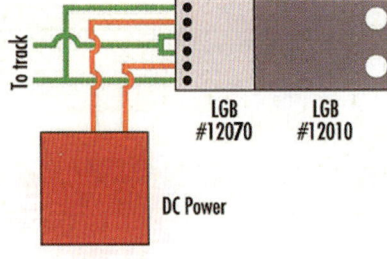

The same components are used here, but the hookups have been changed so that the center taps are connected to the track instead of the power supply. The circuit performs the same, but now if there is a momentary short, power is sent harmlessly to the track instead of back to the power supply.

Fig. 12 Automatic reverse-loop control

depending on the area. These can begin to show more detail, such as trees.

Paint the distant hills across the entire backdrop with light violet or purple paint. Next, paint the closer hills brown or green. As you do this, paint over the distant mountains in some areas and let them show in others. This creates an illusion of distance.

Next, paint in the trees. A tree is easy to do. Paint the trunk first in brown or gray. Then, with a paint brush or a sponge, dab on the foliage in several different shades of green. Liquid acrylic paints work well for painting hills and trees. Remember to go lightly and not overdo the background. Clouds can be added but are not necessary. Don't worry about errors. You can always paint over them.

More detail on reverse loops

Reverse loops, such as on Frank's layout, present electrical problems that must be solved in order to run track-powered trains. I recommend omitting reverse loops in your design if they can be avoided. Anytime you have to run a train through a turnout or depend on something working automatically, you increase chances of trouble.

Having said that, there are some instances where you must use a reverse loop in order to accomplish your goals. This is especially true if you want to run a single-track main line from one point to another but want the option of

continuous operation. If you must use a reverse loop, keep the design as simple as possible and wire it so that it operates automatically.

If you are using a radio-control system, or any system that has a sensitive protection circuit, consider this: You may want to wire the polarity-reversing switch differently from the conventional method shown in the LGB manual (**fig. 12**).

I use a radio-control system, and I have a loop-to-loop railroad. When I wired it for automatic operation, there was a problem. Every so often, when the train crossed the contact that reversed the track polarity, the engine would stop because of a momentary short circuit.

I discussed the problem with my friend Steve Russell (an electrical engineer). After several hours of experimentation, we discovered that the LGB no. 12070 unit did not always switch both contacts at precisely the same time. Occasionally, the contacts would cause a momentary short circuit because they would switch slightly out of synchronization.

After studying the problem, Steve suggested reversing the hookup so that the track leads were connected to the center pole of the no. 12070 switch and the power supply to the outside poles. This solved the problem. Now, if there is a momentary short, it's sent harmlessly to the track, not the power supply.

2

Flat areas on hillsides make good settings for towns. Elevating a town on a hillside makes the structures more visible. The scenery surrounding this future town resembles areas of the Rocky Mountains of Colorado and the gold mountains of California. *Photo by Marc Horovitz*

One end of the garden on Don and Sue Watters's Tahoe & Truckee Railroad in Los Altos, California, features a pond and waterfall. The formal brick-lined pond and bottom half of the waterfall existed before the railroad. The area behind the existing waterfall was built up, and the waterfall was extended all the way up the hill to form a new stream. Using rocks and trees, the new area was tied into the old. The railroad was run around the old waterfall on a trestle, which nicely tied the waterfall and pond into the railroad. The mountain, from which the new stream flows (upper left), is over five feet high.

The railroad used to be at ground level through the lawn. The grass is now free of track, making mowing much easier, and the new Tahoe & Truckee runs in its own area. A boulder retaining wall helps blend the lawn and the railroad. Baby tears were planted in the cracks to soften the appearance of the rocks.

SECTION 5:
Integrating the railroad

There are two basic garden-railroad settings. In one, the railroad has its own place and is an island. No attempt is made to integrate it with the surrounding landscape. A good example of this is Ken Kirkorian's railroad. His railroad was built in a large, raised planter box surrounded by a concrete walkway. Although the cement work blends into other cement features in the yard, the railroad's space is clearly defined.

The second type of setting is the integrated railroad. This railroad runs in either a preexisting landscape or in a landscape that was specifically built for it. In this type of garden railroad, the idea is to blend, or integrate, the railroad with its surroundings.

Integrating the railroad
One of my favorite garden railroads is Don and Sue Watters's Tahoe & Truckee Line. Don started his railroad several years ago as a line that ran on his lawn. He contacted me about designing and building a larger,

improved railroad that would meet his true desires. The Watters's backyard landscaping, a peaceful setting that offers the feel of forested mountains, was professionally designed. One of our goals was to integrate the railroad into this existing landscape.

The old railroad had to go. It was anything but integrated. Being on the grass, the railroad limited the use of the lawn and created mowing problems. In carefully examining the site, we realized that there was a space between the lawn and the fence in which a railroad could be built. This turned out to be a larger area than we realized when we started removing plants and clearing the area for construction.

Since Don's first railroad was on the ground, it was not hard to convince him that an elevated line would be much more fun to operate. After surveying the area, the decision was made to go ahead with the raised railroad.

First, a block retaining wall was built along the fence line, about 18" away from the fence, to allow limited access to the railroad and provide working room to build a new fence when needed. Next, fill dirt was brought in to raise the railroad's area to the desired height. In some places, the railroad landscaping is over six feet high and, at the lowest level, is about 18" off the ground. The basic construction method was to raise the back side of the area with a retaining wall and to make a front wall using natural materials: in this case, boulders.

Blending railroad and landscape

Then came the fun part. Blending the railroad with the existing landscape was fairly easy, since it was built along the fence. The railroad became a natural backdrop for the full-size landscaping. Photos cannot do it justice. Some areas are so well blended you cannot tell where the full-size landscape ends and the railroad begins.

An existing brick mowing strip became a border between the railroad and the lawn. Large landscape boulders were used to form the front retaining wall. Once it was built up, trees were added to the wall to make it look less like a stone wall and more like the beginning of a mountain area with a

Other ways to integrate a garden railroad

The author's Crystal Springs Railroad in San Mateo, California

On my railroad, the gazebo and deck are integrated into the scene by softening their edges. On the right, dwarf Alberta spruce blend the deck into the railroad, while on the left, a cryptomeria hides the end post of the gazebo's railing. The gazebo predates the railroad, so the railroad has grown around it.

An unsightly control box (right) is partially hidden by the addition of a rock formation and trees. The rocks hold the soil in place. Drippers water the trees, so there is little runoff. Notice how the rock formation leads your eye into the railroad area beyond. There are no trains in this area, but the landscaping is similar to the garden railroad's, which prepares you to see more as you walk along.

Other ways to integrate a garden railroad

Anne and Otto Graf's Santa Fe & Kitchen Corner Railroad, Newark, California

The railroad of Anne Graf and her late husband Otto is unique in that it has a variety of railroad settings in one railroad. The backyard, seen here, is fully landscaped.
Photo by Marc Horovitz

The Grafs' front yard is exposed to a lot of pedestrian traffic, so a method for protecting the railroad was devised. What the casual observer sees is a nice front yard with a white picket fence around it. But on weekends, down comes the fence to reveal the railroad! *Photo by Marc Horovitz*

forest. Baby tears, planted between the boulders, soften their lines and blend the lawn with the wall. Even though there is a hard border line (the mowing strip) between the lawn and railroad, the baby tears help integrate the railroad into the landscape without the border being obtrusive.

Rock color was also an important consideration. We used brownish-gray rocks with some reddish tones. These are relatively neutral in color and do not show a clear line of demarcation between the railroad and the full-size landscape. Contrasting colors could be used. For example, gray granite or red cinder would be striking if placed next to a green lawn.

Integrated observation areas

Another form of integration is "integrated observation areas." The Watters's yard had an existing brick patio with several built-in benches, along with freestanding patio chairs and tables. The railroad was built so that parts of it could be viewed while sitting in this area. Don also has a recessed cove in which he can hang a hammock; he can see the train crossing a waterfall from the hammock.

Integrated observation areas can be built more easily into the railroad when you are starting from scratch. With a little imagination, you can come up with some well-concealed—or, I should say, well-integrated—seating areas for observation. Rocks, stumps, or logs can be part of the landscape but can also double as seating areas.

Another way to integrate the railroad into the landscape is for miniature landscaping to extend beyond the actual garden-railroad area. For example, if you have a walkway that goes up to the railroad or runs alongside it, you could add some miniature landscape features on the other side of the path. This creates a sense of harmony between the railroad and the rest of the yard.

In the real world, landscaping does not stop at the tracks. There's no reason to restrict your miniature landscaping to the confines of the railroad space. You can create miniature landscapes outside the garden railroad's operating area to match the landscape.

CHAPTER

3 Groundwork

Strong wooden cribbing is used to retain the earth, providing an abutment for the trestle.

For many, groundwork is the most enjoyable part of a project. Rolling up your sleeves and going to work can feel very rewarding. In this chapter, you'll learn how to create the foundation for your railroad—roadbed. We'll also discuss the use of rock in the garden railway and how it can accent the landscape and railroad.

Roadbed construction

There is an old saying that if you want to keep friends, don't argue politics or religion. A twist on that for our hobby is that if you want to keep friends, don't discuss roadbed or ballast. I have been in garden railroading for more than 20 years, and I've read a lot of articles on roadbed and ballast. I am also sure this will not be the last article you see on the subject, for it seems to be a rich and deep topic for discussion.

If you want a railroad that will survive earthquakes, floods, and the next Ice Age, you might want to build your roadbed out of steel encased in concrete, with pilings every five feet, sunk well below the frost line and tested by the Army Corps of Engineers. This seems to be the mindset of some. Too many people want to do it the hard way! A good rule to follow when building a garden railroad is to use prototype practice wherever possible. This applies here. If your roadbed is done right, you do not need to use concrete or concrete block.

The most important thing about roadbed construction is to create a substructure to retain the ballast and support the track. If you are building the railroad directly on the ground, the earth can serve as this structure.

For ground-level roadbed, dig a trench about 4" or 5" below grade level and about three times wider than the track (**fig. 1**). This trough will hold the subroadbed ballast. If you are creating mountains, you can use boulders to form a plateau, or bed, upon which the roadbed can be built (**fig. 2**). Use the boulders to form a retaining wall that looks like a natural cliff.

You can also use partial trestles, retaining walls, or cribbing to support track and roadbed on side hills (**fig. 3**).

Ballast

I put ballast into two different categories: working ballast and decorative, or finish, ballast.

Working ballast does the real work of supporting the track, trains, and even people. It goes in first and is often covered later by decorative ballast. Decorative, or finish, ballast can be anything you like.

I am very selective as to what I use for working ballast. My material of choice is "gray fines" or the equivalent. This is made up of ¼" and smaller crushed rock. It is sometimes called minus, fines, crusher fines, or quarry waste. In any case, there's a lot of dust and fine material in it. This product, when packed and wetted, sets up almost like concrete, but remains porous and can be easily broken back down to its original state with a pick or other excavating tool. It can be piled up and will hold a 45-degree angle.

The thing that makes ballast work is its mass. Ballast holds the track in place by interlocking around and under the ties. The heavier and denser the ballast, the better it will hold.

The list of materials that should not be used for subroadbed is much longer. Don't use crushed granite, pea gravel, lava rock, aquarium sand, chicken grit, sand, or kitty litter. These materials may look appropriate, but they do not have the interlocking properties or the mass and density that fines have. However, if you like the look of any of these materials, you can use them as decorative ballast on the surface.

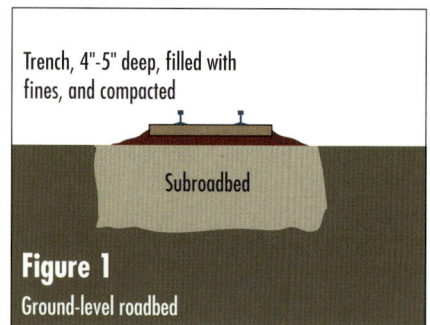

Trench, 4"-5" deep, filled with fines, and compacted

Subroadbed

Figure 1
Ground-level roadbed

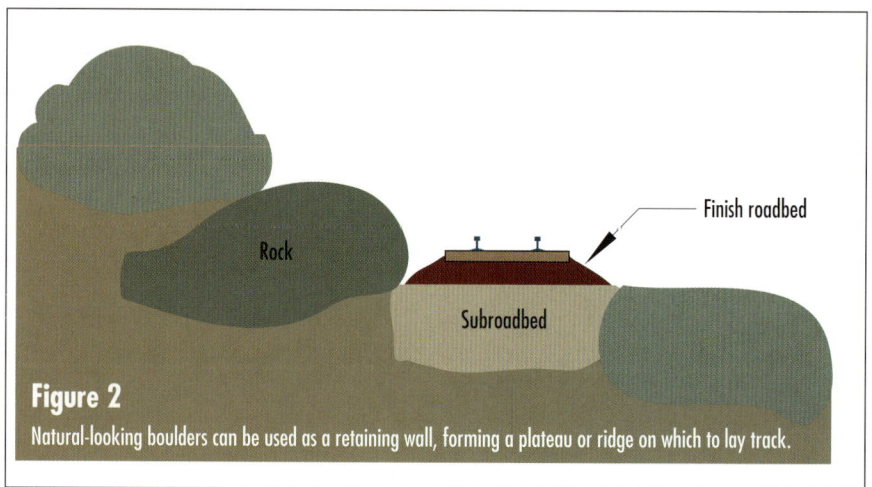

Rock

Finish roadbed

Subroadbed

Figure 2
Natural-looking boulders can be used as a retaining wall, forming a plateau or ridge on which to lay track.

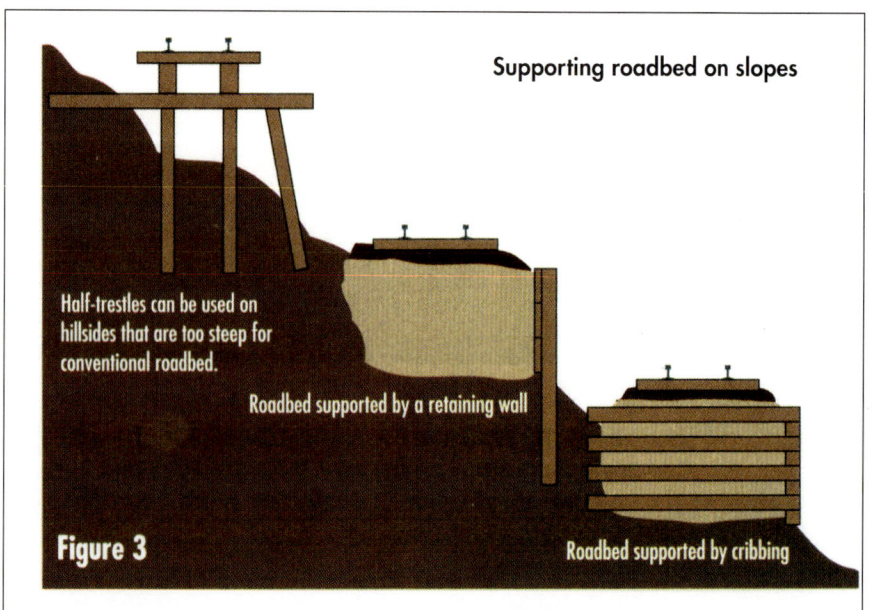

Supporting roadbed on slopes

Half-trestles can be used on hillsides that are too steep for conventional roadbed.

Roadbed supported by a retaining wall

Figure 3

Roadbed supported by cribbing

Decorative ballast

One problem with fines is they are dull and plain to look at. You can use decorative ballast to add color to the line. Decorative ballast, used to finish off the roadbed, is the layer that can be seen. It is applied over the top of the working ballast and is for looks only. Since it is just a surface coating, you will not need much of it.

You can choose from many colors. For example, aquarium sand that has a mixture of colors, such as black, gray, white, and some brown, will offer a cool appearance, while fines that are yellow/gold will give a warm feel, like the desert. In a different setting, gold fines could look like earthen ballast. Red lava rock gives a warm look. Chicken grit is uniformly gray in color but has a nice texture, as does kitty litter.

In real life, a variety of materials are used for ballast, with a wide range of colors. Some railroads spread cinders out over ballast, giving it a black color, while other lines use snow-white rock. The important thing is to use a material that is the right size. If it's too large, the ballast will not do its job, as it will have too many gaps or voids between the rocks. Too small, and the material will wash away. A good size for finish ballast is no. 10, with small rocks about the size of BBs.

Working with ballast

The bulk of the working ballast should be installed before laying track. It can be placed with a shovel. A tamper is used to pack the material down.

Using the grade-stake system (mentioned in chapter 1), fill the roadbed nearly to the top of the stakes with working ballast. Next, tamp the material down. Always tamp the material when it is dry. If wet, the roadbed will stick to the tamper. After the dry material is tamped, you can wet it to help pack it even more.

Next, lay the track. You will see that there will be high and low spots in the ballast. Use the track as a guide for how much ballast to add or remove. The track should be lying on top of the grade stakes. (If you live in a climate where frost heave is a problem, remove the grade stakes before laying the track.) Next, using a material scoop and

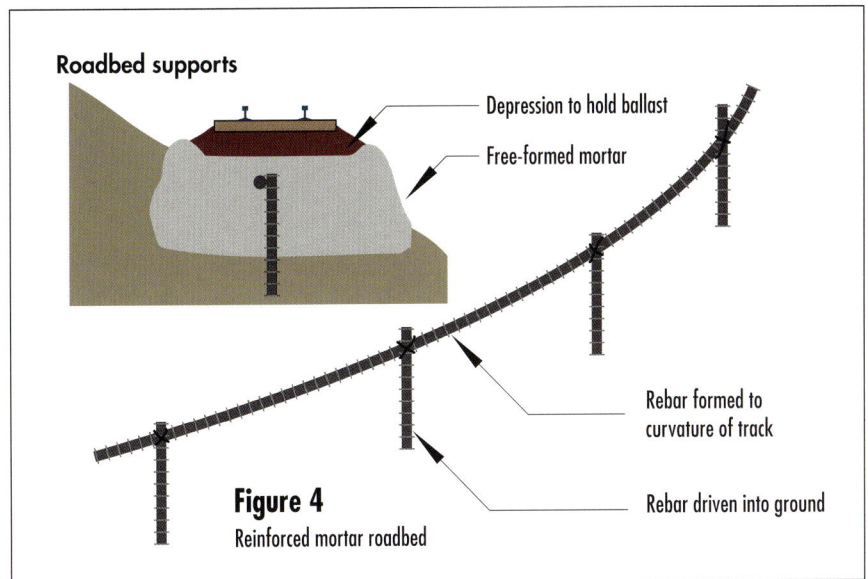

Roadbed supports

Depression to hold ballast

Free-formed mortar

Rebar formed to curvature of track

Rebar driven into ground

Figure 4
Reinforced mortar roadbed

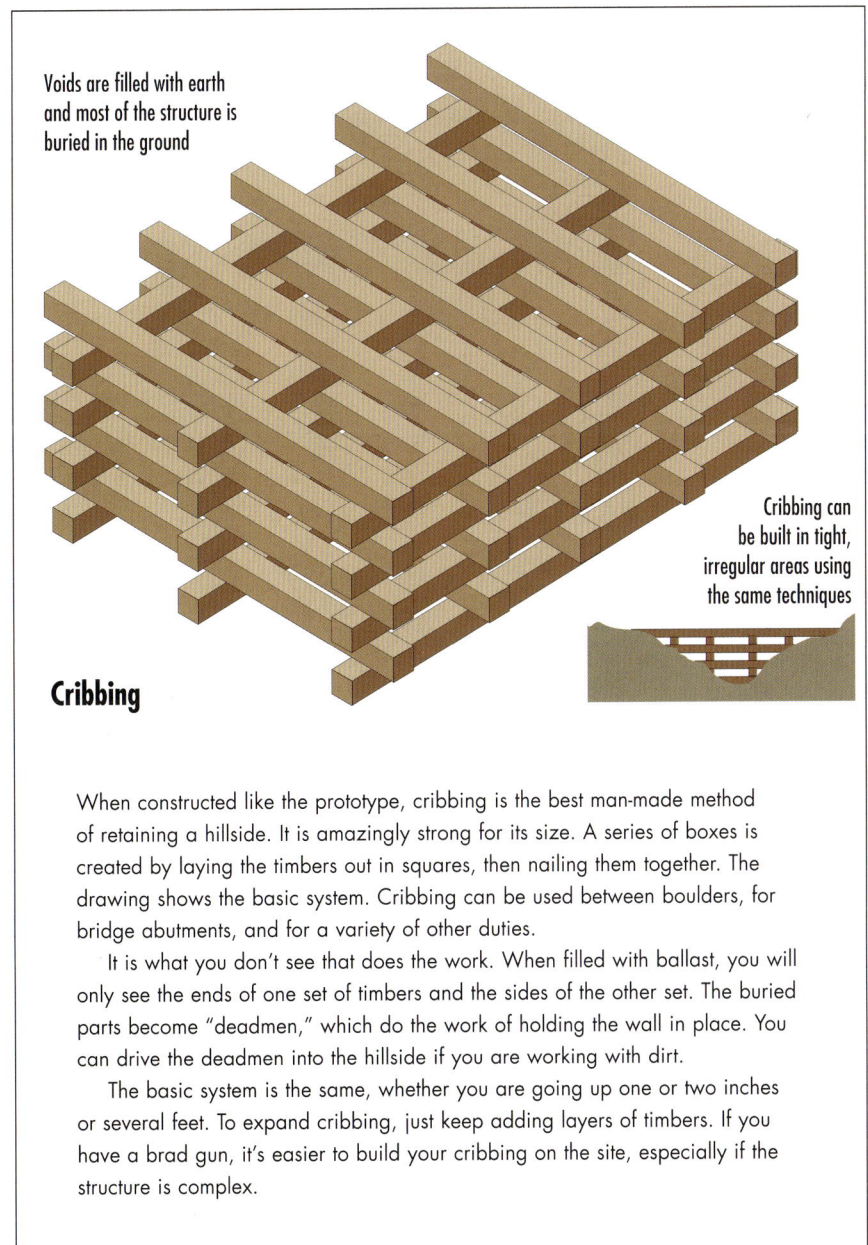

Voids are filled with earth and most of the structure is buried in the ground

Cribbing can be built in tight, irregular areas using the same techniques

Cribbing

When constructed like the prototype, cribbing is the best man-made method of retaining a hillside. It is amazingly strong for its size. A series of boxes is created by laying the timbers out in squares, then nailing them together. The drawing shows the basic system. Cribbing can be used between boulders, for bridge abutments, and for a variety of other duties.

It is what you don't see that does the work. When filled with ballast, you will only see the ends of one set of timbers and the sides of the other set. The buried parts become "deadmen," which do the work of holding the wall in place. You can drive the deadmen into the hillside if you are working with dirt.

The basic system is the same, whether you are going up one or two inches or several feet. To expand cribbing, just keep adding layers of timbers. If you have a brad gun, it's easier to build your cribbing on the site, especially if the structure is complex.

3

a whisk broom or fox-tail brush, start pouring ballast over the track and working it in with the brush or broom. The grade stake will help you keep the track at the proper elevation. Use a torpedo level to level the track from side to side. At this point, you are still using fines.

Next, water the ballast. This should be done over a few days, "wetting in" the roadbed a little more each day. You will notice that the ballast material will settle a little, creating small voids that should be filled.

Now you can use your choice of decorative ballast to finish the job. Be aware that the ballast will settle over time. As it settles, you can continue to add your choice of decorative ballast until that is all you see. If there are areas that have settled excessively, add more working ballast. A roadbed is like a fine wine. It needs to be aged and gets better with time.

The main advantage of this system is that the roadbed is flexible and is easily rebuilt. It can move with the ground. If the ground sinks, just add more ballast.

This is what prototype railroads do. The secret is using the right working ballast.

Using a weed block, such as landscape fabric, is a waste of time. Weeds will grow in your ballast with or without weed block. A problem with a weed block is that it acts as a barrier between the ballast and the earth, which prevents the ballast from locking to the earth.

This is the same problem with cement subroadbed, and roadbeds such as pavers (special sidewalk bricks). The ballast does not lock to the surface of the cement and will slide around too much. Ballast is meant to hold the track in position from right to left as well as in the horizontal plane.

A concrete roadbed may be needed in some cases. For this, I use a free-form method using mortar and rebar (metal bar used for reinforcing concrete).

Drive the rebar into the ground in the same way you would install a grade stake. Next, form a piece of rebar to the track curvature. Wire the rebar together, forming a spine under the track (**fig. 4**). Next, mix a batch of mortar and spread it over the rebar to form a roadbed. When the mortar has cured, the rebar will lock the roadbed together.

While the mortar is still workable, spread finish ballast over it and work it in to create an exposed-aggregate look. If you need to add additional finish ballast to the roadbed later, it can be applied using concrete adhesive.

Do not anchor the track to the roadbed! In almost all cases, track should not be fastened in any way to the roadbed. The ballast will hold the track in position. This is how you allow for expansion and contraction, as the track actually slides around a little in the ballast.

Finishing touches
Looking at prototype railroad roadbed, you will notice that it is really a very narrow band crossing the landscape. When building your roadbed, employ the working ballast liberally, using as much as you need to support the roadbed. When you are done, dress the edges with soil or plant materials to create that narrow band, just like a full-size railroad.

These tools, except for the long pry bar, are the basic tools for building and maintaining roadbed: 1. Six-inch-square tamper. 2. Mason's wooden float. 3. Plastic torpedo level. 4. Drywall sander. 5. Gong brush mounted on a broom handle. 6. Gong brush. 7. Counter brush (foxtail). 8. Whisk broom. 9. Shrubbery rake. 10. Pry bar. 11. Trenching shovel.

3

Miniature landscaping with natural materials: Introduction

When I discovered this hobby, a whole new world opened up to me. The challenge of creating realistic settings for the trains using natural material eventually became a major interest.

A natural extension of this new-found interest was landscaping. A funny twist in the road of life came when I decided I wanted to build garden railways for other people. In California, you have to be licensed as a contractor to work on others' property. So, as a result of my hobby interest, I became a licensed landscape contractor. Over the years, I have developed a real love of miniature landscaping. I believe a well-designed garden railway will stand on its own as a beautiful landscape, even without the train. Most of the time, you see the landscape without the train running, even if you run your trains a lot. So it is worth the effort to make landscaping a high priority in your overall plan.

I have strong preferences when it comes to landscaping. I like mountains, water, and rolling countryside, and I like green hills and trees. Please understand if I don't cover flatland areas and colorful flowers here.

The basic concept in landscaping is to create a scene you will enjoy, one that is pleasing to the eye. Garden-railroad landscaping shares many things with Japanese-style gardens. One of these ideas is to try to make a space look larger by using small features, such as miniature plants and rocks. When done right, your yard can look much larger than it really is.

An introduction to landscaping materials

Before you begin to build your miniature landscape, you need to learn about available materials. Those that will be discussed in this book are the building blocks of your garden railroad landscape. Some of the materials may be called by different names in your area.

This rock outcropping on the author's garden railway was constructed with head- and double-head-size stones. Ground cover has helped make these well-planted rocks look like they have been there for millions of years.

Even in my area, each supplier has a different name for the same rock. With that in mind, I will try to describe the characteristics of each material and show a photo of each one so you will know what to look for. My goal is to give you enough information to choose the right rock for the job.

Because materials go by different names, you should always see them before you buy. For example, in my area, if you call three different rock yards and ask for moss rock, you'll probably get three different types of rocks.

Rock

Rock is one of the mainstays of garden-railroad construction. Not only is it part of the structure of the landscape, but stone contributes to the overall look and mood of the railroad.

An infinite variety of rocks will work in a garden railroad. The choice is a matter of personal preference. I'll describe the types of rocks I believe work best in creating a believable miniature landscape.

If stone is to be used as fill or as sub-roadbed, it does not matter what it looks like, since it will be buried.

However, if you are going to use the rock to form visible landscaping, then it should be a good-looking variety.

Stone varies from region to region. This is true both with the rocks that are found in the natural landscape and those that are available at local rock yards and landscape-materials stores. These may not be available in your area, or they may be called by different names, but I think the general rules in rock use can be applied to any selection.

General landscape rocks for use in making mountains

My first consideration in choosing rock is its overall appearance. This includes two primary attributes. First, and most important, is shape and texture; second is color.

Size is another consideration. Generally speaking, larger rocks work better for making mountains. I usually use rocks that are head and double-head size. Head and double-head are terms used to indicate the size of a rock. As implied, "head size" is about the size of a human head. Double-head is twice as big. These are sizes that can be manhandled.

3

If larger rocks are used, special machinery may be required to handle them. Anything larger than double-head size should be carefully selected with a specific application in mind. It's easier to make rock formations out of smaller rocks than out of huge rocks. If you have a yard with limited access, the size and weight of the rocks you select present a more practical problem. Can you get them into your yard? If they have to be carried a long way, weight will be an important consideration.

It is interesting how much weight difference there is between various types of stone of equal dimensions. As an example, holey wall rock is much lighter than fieldstone. When you're at the rock yard, pick up and carry a sample of your rock (or rocks) of choice to see how easy or difficult it will be to move them around. A good tool for moving large rocks is a two-wheel hand truck with pneumatic tires (shown below). Smaller rocks can be moved easily in a wheelbarrow.

SECTION 3:
Miniature landscaping with natural materials: Rock types and shapes

When examining rocks, visualize how they will appear if viewed from a scale prospective. Individually, some rocks might look like mountains in miniature. Other rocks, working together, can make formations like those found on a cliffside or in an area that has been blown or cut away to make the roadbed of a railroad or highway.

Irregular rocks
I prefer rocks with irregular shapes, ones that have natural crevices, small holes, and rough forms, such as "roping." Roping is a twisted strata that

◀ Large rocks that must be moved with heavy equipment should be chosen for specific situations on the railway, like this one, where a huge stone is used as a mesa on Barb and Marc Horovitz's Ogden Botanical Railway. *Photo by Marc Horovitz*

▼ Double-head-size (and sometimes even larger) rocks can be moved with a two-wheel hand truck. *Photo by Marc Horovitz*

looks like rope or eroded earth. You may find a variety of other interesting features in a pile of rock.

My favorite rock is a type called holey wall rock. It may also be called by other names, such as mossy wall rock. Holey wall rock contains many small holes and comes in all kinds of shapes and sizes. The particular variety I use looks like volcanic rock but is not as light as pumice. Our local variety is usually mossy. I like it for its variety in texture and shape. Also, because these rocks are not round, they will interlock with each other, making them structurally suitable for miniature mountain building. The ultimate find is a rock with one flat side.

Fieldstone comes in many types. It is generally not as rough as holey wall rock but still works well for mountains. Fieldstone is a good rock from which to make walls. It's heavy and somewhat uniform in shape. The photos on page 44 show two types of fieldstone available in my area—Napa and Sonoma. These are similar, but upon close examination you will notice that the Napa fieldstone is more irregular in

▲ Feather rock is an amazing material, as it can be carved, cut, and shaped. Feather rock will also accept dye, so it can be colored if you don't like gray.

Flat lava rock is useful for service walkways. It comes in sizes ranging from less than a square foot to as large as 10 square feet. Its darker color makes it blend well with holey wall rock or other similar-color rock. Flat lava rocks can also be placed on edge to form a steep canyon wall or the edge of a railroad cut.

shape, making it a better choice for mountain building, while Sonoma is a little more uniform in shape, which makes it a better choice for walls. Both are heavier than holey wall rock.

Flat rocks

Flat rocks are another basic shape that can be useful in garden-railway landscaping. There are several types of flat rock available.

Green basalt is a heavy rock that can be used for fill. It can also be used to create large rock formations in a miniature landscape.

Holey wall rock is the author's favorite rock. It is versatile, and its irregular shape can be used to create interesting rock formations, either standing alone or used together with others rocks to make a larger formation.

Napa fieldstone has some strata. It is smoother and heavier than holey wall rock and is the author's second choice for making mountains. Napa fieldstone generally has a more irregular shape than Sonoma fieldstone (seen in the photo at right), making Napa a better choice for mountain building.

Sonoma fieldstone, also known as Sonoma wall rock, is a common fieldstone. It is basically round, with some strata, and is most useful as wall rock. The main advantages of Sonoma (and Napa) wall rock over others are its weight and uniform shape. These are pluses when it comes to building a wall, but disadvantages when making a mountain or other landscape feature.

Flagstone is usually tan in color, although many other colors are available. This flat rock can be as thin as ½" and has an almost-smooth texture. Flagstone is normally used to make walkways and patios. In a garden railroad, it can be used to create mountains by flat-stacking it, which gives you horizontal strata.

Flat lava and Cold Water Canyon

These are local names for another class of flat rock that may be called by other names in your area. The stones have more texture than flagstone and so are not as suitable for walkway use. They can be used to make horizontal strata, or they can be used to form mountainsides by setting them upright, so that one edge is in the ground. The flat side then becomes the mountainside. This method makes for nice rock formations along the tracks, especially at tunnel openings or in simulated cuts.

Round rocks

Round rocks and smooth rocks, such as river rocks, are generally not suitable for miniature mountains. I call these "goose eggs." In real life, these are commonly found in riverbeds and around ancient glacial flows. They are usually off-white or gray in color, but occur in other colors, too. In proportion to the garden-railway landscape, they are much too large to use for most landscape features. They can be used as fill, however, so if you have an abundance of these rocks on your property, they do not have to go to waste.

Smaller sizes of round rock can be used in dry washes. In order to make

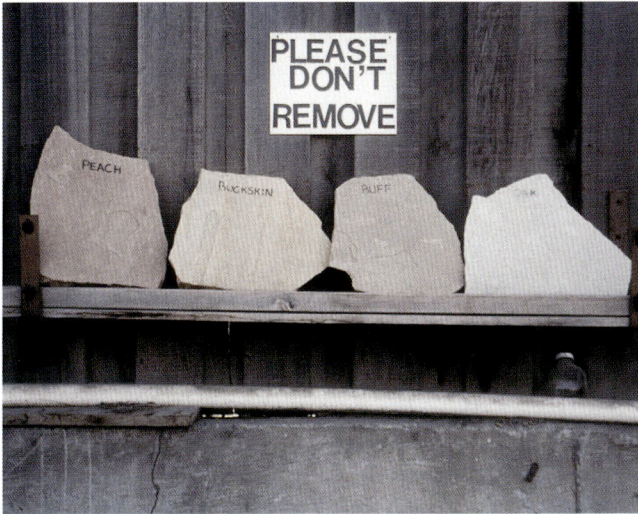

Peach, buckskin, buff, and oak flagstone are useful for stepping stones and in dry washes. They are relatively smooth and can also be stacked horizontally for a rock face.

Water-washed flagstone looks good when stacked horizontally. This size is a little large to be used in a scale stream bed.

Cold Water Canyon (CWC) is an interesting bi-colored rock. One side is reddish brown, and the other is dark brown with some black. CWC can be used as stepping stones, but it can get slippery, since it's relatively smooth and is usually crowned. It is best used for dry washes or as part of a rock face when stacked horizontally. Since it is crowned and has some strata, it can be used on edge as a rock face.

Gnarly boulder is just one of many specialty rocks. This particular stone could make a mountain all by itself. Look for other types of specialty rocks in nature as well as at landscape supply dealers.

them look like part of a riverbed, you may have to bury half or more of each stone so that only a little bit shows above ground.

Another technique is to break these rocks into smaller pieces to provide some rough working edges. In some areas in the full-size world, you can find large, round stones that have been deposited by ancient glaciers. So, if you really want to use round rocks, they can be placed in a manner that imitates an ancient glacial flow. That being said, I prefer not to use round rocks at all,

since it takes a lot of effort to make them look natural. I would not recommend buying this kind of rock. I mention it here only because many people will find these on their property.

Specialty rock

Many special rocks are available in rock yards and in nature. Choose these carefully. You should have a mental picture of where and how you will place them. Sometimes a rock looks interesting by itself, but it might not look good integrated into the landscape.

Feather rock is a most interesting volcanic rock. In fact, it is actually glass. It is, as its name implies, very lightweight. Its other interesting feature is that it can be cut and split with relative ease and can also be carved.

Using an electric jackhammer with a chisel blade, you can quickly split these rocks. This can also be done by hand with a hammer and chisel, for those who like to do things the old-fashioned way. In either case, do not allow the chisel to go too deeply into the rock or it could become embedded. A series of

Desert cloud is a specialty fieldstone. This material looks good sitting in the rock yard, but how will it look in your railway's landscape? Plan how you are going to use it. It can be stacked horizontally or placed vertically.

New England wall rock is a flat, gray stone with rounded edges. Since it does not have a lot of strata, it would probably look best stacked horizontally.

many shallow cuts will do the trick. These rocks can also be carved with a reciprocating saw (such as a Sawzall) or a hatchet. I have actually cut tunnel openings through this type of rock.

The main advantage in splitting these rocks is that you end up with one flat side, which will make a good base or bottom. The main disadvantage to feather rock is that it is very sharp when freshly quarried or cut. Some of the sharpness erodes with time, but it can still tear your skin if you fall on it or grab it the wrong way. When handling feather rock, always wear gloves, elbow pads (or long sleeves), and eye protection.

Color-wise, you are limited to tones of gray and some beige. I have found, though, that you can color it with concrete dye. Feather rock is so porous it will absorb the dye. This rock will change color over time because it absorbs dirt and other debris that comes in contract with it.

Mexican bowl rock is a volcanic stone that has many irregular edges and depressions. Desert rose is a reddish-brown rock that is very rough and comes in long, skinny pieces that work very well for desert rock formations. These rocks can be used to enhance water features.

Visit rock yards near you to see what they offer. Look at everything before making decisions and, if you are unsure, make several trips after closely evaluating the needs of your railway.

SECTION 4:
Miniature landscaping with natural materials: Small rock and gravel

Small rock

A variety of small rock materials range in size from ¼" to ¾". These are considered gravel or sand, but in our small world, these sizes can be used as small boulders, broken rocks, or, in dry washes and streambeds, as water-washed rock. Some can be used as decorative ballast. However, I would not recommend these materials for working ballast, since they do not interlock or pack down.

Pea gravel comes in ¼" to ⅜" sizes. It can be used for walkways, riverbeds, and as chips that have fallen from larger rock (always found at the base of large rock formations). Pea gravel is also useful for drainage. I recommend using it for ballast in tunnels, where you do not need interlocking materials (since the ballast is confined by the tunnel walls), but where you do need free-flowing drainage.

Aquarium sand is a clean, washed sand that has a nice mixture of colors in black, white, and gray tones. I like to use it as decorative ballast. Aquarium sand is perfect for river and streambeds and pond bottoms. In fact, it is river rock in miniature. It can also be used in tunnels, since it drains well. (Another use for this material is in pond filters.)

Quartz is a light-colored rock that has potential to make a good base for a water feature.

La Paz rock is normally used for exposed aggregate in patios. It has a lot of color.

Lin Creek, in its smaller size, makes a good base for water features.

Red or brown lava rock (¼", ⅜", ½") is useful as a soil amendment. It helps keep the soil loose so water can penetrate. In some cases, you can use this smaller rock as mulch to cover bare soil, either temporarily until ground cover is planted, or permanently in place of living ground cover. Later, if you want to add live ground cover, just mix planting soil with the lava rock and plant it. I like to call lava rock the "zero" of landscaping. In math, a zero is a placeholder. This is what the lava rock is—a placeholder until you decide what you are going to do permanently. One other advantage of lava rock is that it absorbs the energy of falling rain or water from a sprinkler, helping to control soil erosion.

Rock debris. A common way to buy rock is in large wire baskets. A couple of by-products of loading and unloading rocks into these carriers are rock chips and mossy scraps. These rock chips can be used to imitate broken rock that has fallen from a larger rock formation, and the moss from chips can be transplanted.

When planting a rock for use as an outcropping, its base should be buried so the rock looks like it is part of the landscape and not just lying on the ground. Here, ground cover helps these rocks look like they have been there for millions of years.

La Paz is a colorful mix of gray tones that makes a good rock for dry washes as well as streambeds.

Half-inch Salmon Bay is a pebble with varied shading that matches the color of gold fines.

Crushed rock

As the name implies, crushed rock is made from larger rock that has been crushed into various sizes. This material is useful for many things, including subroadbeds, ballast, fill material, roadways, and bases under buildings.

Another use is as broken rock that has fallen off of larger rocks at the base of a large formation. You can find crushed rock in a variety or colors, like gold, gray, blue, and even a shade of green. Crushed rock in larger sizes is also useful for drainage.

Crushed granite can be used as small boulders in conjunction with large granite boulders or with feather rock. It can also be used as decorative ballast or ballast inside tunnels. Crushed granite is usually found in three sizes: ¼", ½", and ¾". In some

Quarter-inch pea gravel is useful as either decorative ballast or drain rock. It is cheaper, smoother, and darker than crushed granite.

Quarter-inch Pami pebble can be used in a dry wash.

Quarter-inch quartz is a light-colored aggregate. It is often too bright for use in a garden railway.

Gold fines are small crushed rocks, sometimes called decomposed granite. The section below the shovel has been tamped. Fines can be made smooth for roadways or left rough.

Red lava is available in many sizes. This product can be used as a soil amendment to help keep soil loose and allow water to penetrate.

Gray fines are best used for subroadbed and working ballast. Gray fines work well for ballast because they pack hard, almost like cement. After packing, wet it down to help it set.

places you can buy no. 10 crushed granite, sometimes called chicken grit. This makes a nice, decorative ballast.

Drain rock is less expensive. It is common rock that has been broken into smaller pieces (¾" is best for drainage). It can also be used as miniature fieldstone in landscaping.

Fines are similar to crushed rock, except they have been reduced to pieces

that are usually ¼" or smaller. The finished product is not washed, thus includes dust in the mix. Fines are especially good for ballast, roads, and bases for miniature buildings.

Blue and gray fines are monochrome materials that aren't particularly pretty, so are not necessarily good material for decorative landscaping. However, blue and gray fines do make

excellent fill material. The material compacts quickly and does not take as long to settle as common fill dirt does.

Gold fines or **gold dust**, also sometimes called decomposed granite, is a fines material with color. Its yellow-gold tone makes it ideal for use in miniature roadways that you want to look like dirt roads. It can also be used as tailings around mines.

▲ This rock face was made of holey wall rock, used because it looks like eroded soil or broken rock. The outcropping serves as both an erosion-control device and a decorative part of the landscape. Smaller stones at the base simulate broken rocks that have fallen over the years. Also note the moss and lichen on the rocks.

SECTION 5:
Miniature landscaping with natural materials: Working with rock

In making mountains, rocks serve two purposes. One is visual: Rocks give the appearance of rugged outcroppings and stone faces. Their second function is to hold the mountain up. So, when using rocks in making a mountain, you must keep two things in mind: Make sure the good face of the rock is showing, and install the rock in such a way that it supports the structure.

In choosing which side to show, you must use your own judgment. I look for interesting features, such as crevices and other textures. If the rocks have moss, you'll probably want that showing. However, don't let moss be the only determining factor. You can always get moss to grow if you choose the non-mossy side (as explained in the sidebar on moss on page 51).

Using rock for support takes a little thought. You need to interlock the rocks to form a structure that will be held together by gravity. The sequence I use is called "dirt-rock-trees." You stack up dirt, place a rock, and plant a tree.

Here's how it works. If you simply piled up dirt to make a mountain, you'd need a large area at the base to support a tall mountain. By using rocks, you can make a taller mountain in less space because the rock will support the dirt and prevent it from spreading. I set the rocks in place in such a way that the rock wants to roll back into the mountain, sort of pivoting on its bottom side. I balance the rock with one hand to keep it from rolling into the mountain, then back fill behind and under it with soil. This tendency of the rock to roll back into the mountain ensures that gravity will hold it in place permanently. If this is not done, the rock may pop out later due to the weight of the soil behind it or the flow of draining water.

I plant the trees at this time because I like to stack the rocks close. Planting later would be more difficult because the rocks will be too close to each other. I have always been impressed by trees in the mountains that seem to grow right out of rock. By stacking rocks closely together and planting the tree in between, this can be replicated.

As you build up rocks from side to side, interlock the ends of the individual stones. This helps to hold them in place. As you go, step the next rock back a little so it wants to fall back into the mountain. When done this way, it should be difficult to pull a rock out of place with your bare hands. Even though we are building a mountain, we are using wall-building techniques. What makes the structure look like a mountain is the use of trees. When constructing a mountain, leave some space for soil to plant ground cover.

Color is another important consideration. I rank it second only because you can change a rock's color if desired. Natural rock can be found in just about any color you can imagine. However, you should be careful here. Sometimes

▲ San Pedro pebbles were used for this dry wash. The canyon walls are made of a combination of holey wall rock, Cold Water Canyon, and Napa fieldstone. Rocks in a waterway or dry wash are often much lighter in color than the surrounding rocks. Note the use of forced perspective. The dry wash tapers and turns, making it appear longer and larger than it really is.

something that looks striking in real life may look out of place in a miniature setting. For this reason, I tend to use rock with less vivid colors. I try for an overall "look." For example, I want viewers to see a mountainside, not a group of individual rocks. Therefore, I use rocks of similar color to form a larger formation that looks like it might be one piece.

Color also sets mood or feeling. More subdued colors look cooler and may give the feeling of a rain forest or coastal wooded mountains. On the other hand, brighter colors, such as red, may lend a desert feeling to the landscape. Or, when used with trees, you may get the feeling of being in the San Juan Mountains.

Color carries over to ballast as well. Gray ballast looks cooler, while gold or red ballast looks warmer. All of these colors and more are found in the full-size world.

In nature, you may find an odd-color rock in the midst of a larger formation. You must determine if a similar rock in miniature will enhance your mountain's appearance or distract from it. Multi-color rocks work well for Southwest desert-looking landscapes. Here, color is what distinguishes the landscaping. In this case, brighter colors are appropriate.

A word of caution: Sometimes multi-color rocks look great at the rock yard, but when you get home and try to work them into your landscape, you find they just don't look right. Try picking up several samples first to see how they look in your setting.

Coloring rocks

It is always best to find rocks that are naturally the color you want. However, this is not always possible. Sometimes you will find a rock with just the right texture and strata, but the wrong color.

There are several ways to color rock. One is with cans of spray paint. To make the rock look right, just dust on the paint. Spray from a distance and use several colors. For example, along with brown, you might dust on a little black or some beige. Most real rocks aren't one pure color, but instead are a subtle blend of colors. The secret is to spray lightly and mix the colors.

A natural-looking color can be achieved with powdered concrete dye. Paint the rock with a clear coat of lacquer or acrylic sealer. This will give the dye something to stick to. Sprinkle on the dry powder while the sealer is still wet, or mix it with water and spray it on when the rock is dry. The result will be a dry, powdery finish that looks natural. This finish can be sealed with a clear coating, if you like.

Dry washes, canyons, and draws

One concept in miniature landscaping is to create the illusion of space. The following techniques will help to reinforce this effect. When laying out a dry wash, box canyon, or draw, taper it so that it is smaller at the end farthest from the viewer. Another technique is to curve the feature so that its origin is hidden. This makes it look like it goes on beyond the bend. On the floor of the canyon or wash, use larger rocks in front and smaller ones in back. This adds to the illusion of distance.

When stacking flat stones, they should be laid much like bricks—that is, with staggered joints. Use heavy soil, such as topsoil, as fill between and behind the rocks. To economize on materials, you can break the flat rock into smaller pieces, since only the edges will show.

Using flat stone as a rock face

In some cases, you may want to take flat rock and set it on edge so the flat side becomes a rock face. This works well with rocks like Cold Water Canyon and flat lava rock, because they have some strata. Rocks like flagstone are smooth and may not be the best choice for this application.

A typical use of rock in this manner would be where you have cut into the natural hillside, leaving bare dirt. If left to nature, the dirt will eventually erode onto the track. You can use a flat rock to help stabilize the cut. To anchor it, dig a slit trench in which to set the bottom edge of the rock. Then backfill behind the rock, packing the soil. This provides a foundation and prevents the rock from moving.

If you are dealing with extreme conditions, you might want to use mortar instead of soil to anchor the rock. The method is similar. Dig the trench, but also cut into the hillside to make pockets for the mortar. Drive rebar into the pockets, then fill the pockets with mortar. Coat the entire area of dirt with mortar. Brush a coating of concrete adhesive on the backside of the rock, then layer it with mortar as well, and push it into place. This is semi-permanent. You may want to try the non-mortar method first, since it can be changed more easily and will usually work fine.

Flat rock can also be used to line pond edges. The edge of the pond liner can be held in place with flat rocks. Use mortar to blend flat rock into the pond's sides, which will create a cliff-like appearance.

A wide variety of mosses and lichens can be found growing on rocks. This adds a great deal to their overall appearance.

Moss for your rocks

Years ago, I heard that if you put buttermilk on a rock, moss would grow. I could never get this to work. I kept painting my rocks with buttermilk, but the only result was stinky rocks.

Then I read in a garden catalog that you have to harvest moss, put it in a blender with buttermilk, then paint it on the rocks. This method does work, but I found another way.

I harvest some moss by carefully scraping it off rocks in the wild, then I use buttermilk to "glue" the harvested moss to rocks on my railway. After that, I make sure it stays wet. Now the rock has moss on it. Note, though, that this technique will not grow moss in areas where moss is not normally found. Moss will only grow in the right conditions of shade and water, and is often dormant in dry seasons.

Planting or placing rocks on the ground

If you place rocks on the ground to represent mountains, or if you're setting up stones to look like a rock outcropping in a meadow, here are some hints. To make a rock look like part of the landscape, and to give it age, bury part of it in the ground. For this reason, a rock with a flat side is a nice find. Another trick to make a rock look natural is to add smaller pieces of stone around its base to represent bits of rock that have broken off over time. A variety of materials can be used for this. You can break up rocks or use small pieces of lava rock or crushed rock.

In some cases, you can use this smaller rock as mulch to cover bare soil, either temporarily until ground cover is planted, or permanently in the place of living ground cover. I have done both successfully. In places where it is difficult to grow ground cover, I have used crushed rock instead. And, if you decide to plant ground cover later on, you just have to mix soil in with the crushed rock.

In some areas of the country (around Mount Shasta, for instance), you may see boulders that have wound up in a field through a volcanic eruption. In these places, rock will just be lying in a field with nothing built up around the base. To achieve this effect, you may want to use small rocks, such as ½" lava rock. Glacial rocks can be simulated with small, smooth rocks.

▲ To form this natural-looking cut, flat rocks were set on edge. Stone cuts like this are often found at the mouths of tunnels. Note the outcroppings in the foreground, where larger stones have been mostly buried. Once the ground cover has taken hold, the stones look like they've been there for eons.

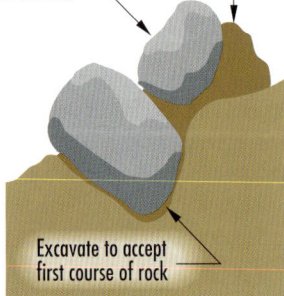

Second and each succeeding course is set so it wants to roll into the hill.

Place fill dirt and soil behind to properly position rock.

Excavate to accept first course of rock

Mountain building with rocks

The first course set in the ground becomes the foundation. The second is laid so that it wants to roll back into the hill. Gravity will hold it in place. Miniature trees should be planted as the mountain is being built, which will help hold it together.

Dirt

You might think that dirt is dirt, but there are actually several kinds to consider when building a landscape. Clean fill is dirt (or other material) that can be used as fill. This is the cheapest dirt. It should be free of organic waste, such as roots, leaves, pine needles, and scrap wood. Materials that can be used as clean fill include fill sand, dirt excavated from swimming pools or building foundations, and broken concrete. Plan so that fill material will be low enough that you will not be digging into it later.

Topsoil or sandy loam (sometimes called heavy soil) is a high-quality fill soil to be used over clean fill and as a sub-layer for nursery mix or planting soil. The main advantage of this material is that it's free of rocks and clods. It can be easily formed and will pack down faster (and is less expensive) than nursery mix or planting mix.

Nursery mix or planting soil is topsoil that has had amendments added, such as compost, chicken manure, horticultural-grade lava, sand, or other additives. Every store will have its own formula. In all cases, this is the top of the line when it comes to dirt. Ideally, you should have at least 12" of planting mix for miniature trees; less is required for low-growing ground covers. This should be placed over a sub-layer of topsoil. The problem with using too much of this good soil is settling. Because it has so many amendments in

Bad

Good

Better

Setting rock into the ground

A more natural look can be realized by burying the bottom of the rock, making it look like it has been in place for centuries. Adding smaller or crushed rocks around the base helps to achieve this look.

Rocks are staggered, like bricks

Stacking flat rock

Laid flat-side down, flat rock can be stacked to look like a rock formation or a mountainside with horizontal strata. Rocks should be set in place at a slight angle to help hold them in place. The first course should be full size (about 12" deep). The second and following courses can be broken, to get more coverage. Use full-depth rocks every few courses for strength and stability.

Use soil to fill the gaps. Sedums and other succulents make excellent plantings in this type of structure, since there is less planting area than there would be when using other types of rock.

Backfill

Full size

Broken

Full size

Backfill with soil

Lean the rock toward the hillside

Setting a flat stone on edge to form a rock face

In most cases, the dug footing will hold just fine. For a heavier installation, use mortar instead of soil. Drive rebar into the soil before pouring the mortar. This will help hold everything together.

Dig down to make a footing

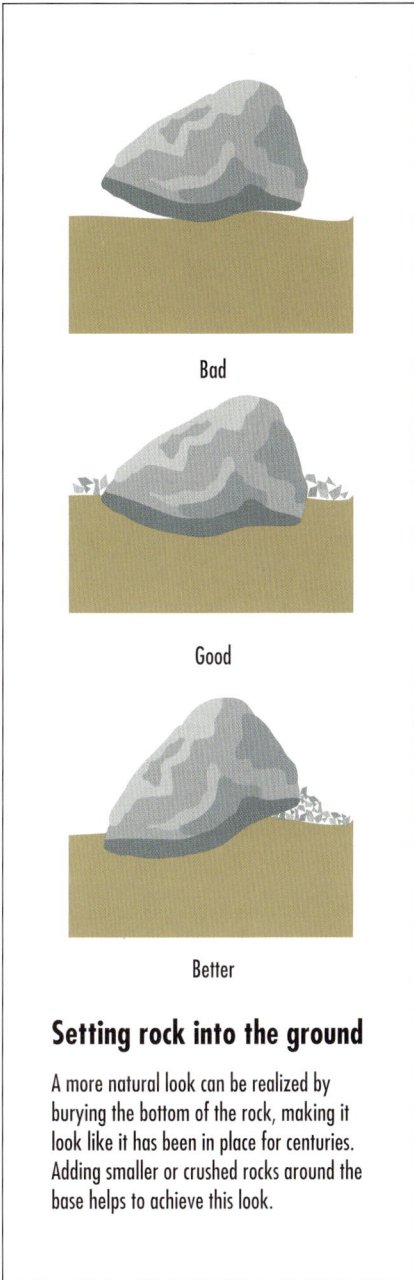

it, it will eventually decompose further and also pack down more.

Your landscape should start with clean fill at the bottom. Form the basic features with this material. Next, cover the clean fill with a layer of topsoil, then finish with planting mix and rocks. The rocks are your erosion control. Plant trees between the rocks as you set them in the landscape. To finish, fill the voids with small crushed rock, such as ⅜" lava or crushed granite (in a color close to the rocks), or plant ground cover.

Screening and road building

If you are using fines to make a road, a good trick you can use is to screen

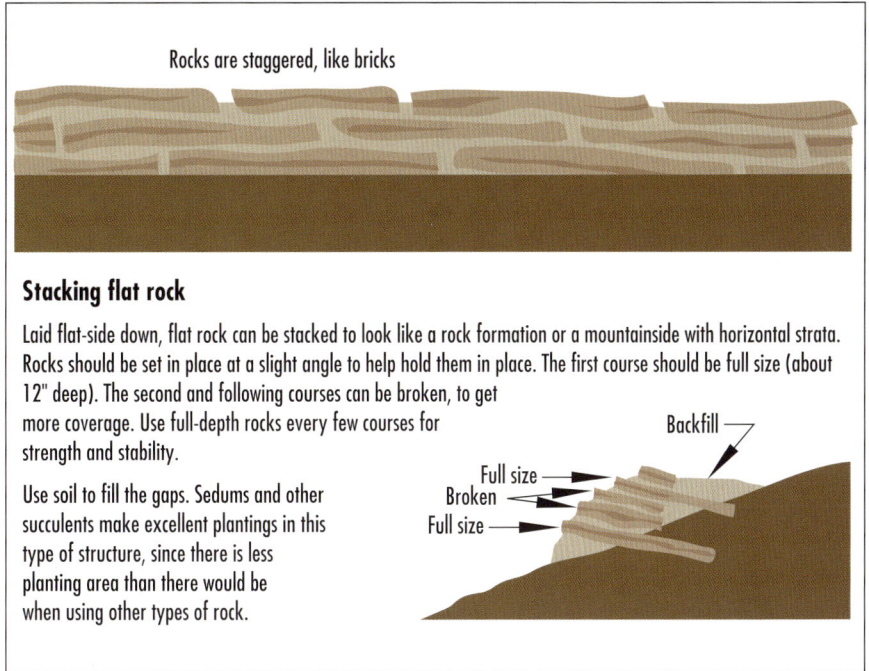

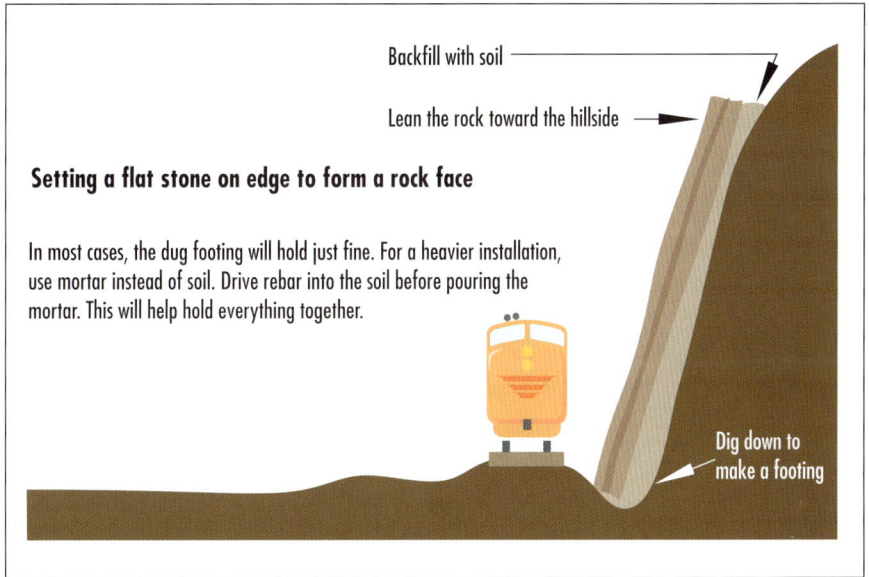

down the material. This can be done using a piece of hardware cloth with spacing about ¼". Place the screen over a bucket, then scoop the fines onto it and sift them through the screen. You will end up with a smooth, uniform material that can be dry-troweled (I like to use a wooden float) directly onto the ground or over a base coat to create a believable roadway.

These fines can be held in place by spraying them with a mixture of concrete adhesive and water (25 percent adhesive, 75 percent water, and a few drops of dish soap to help the mix soak into the fines). This adhesive mix will lock the material in place. This works

best if the sifted fines are installed over a firm base and the fines are not too thick. If your roadway has to be built up, you can use a little Portland cement mixed with the fines (20 percent cement, 80 percent fines) as a base. Dry-mix the fines and cement, apply it to the ground, then lightly spray it with water that has a few drops of dish soap added to it. A spray bottle or garden sprayer can be used to do this. The sifted fines can be applied over this base. If you are gluing the fines to a base coat, brush adhesive onto the base for added strength. As a final touch, make ruts by running wheels over the finish coat before it sets up.

Laying track

Now that you've designed your railway and built the roadbed, it's time to lay some track. When track is properly laid, it will give you many years of reliable service outdoors. This chapter will show you the basics of this important task.

Broad, sweeping curves, like those seen here on Betty and Jud Swedberg's railroad in Northern California, are easily attainable using the methods described in this chapter. *Photo by Marc Horovitz*

Trackwork

A wide variety of track is available today, and which type is best for you depends on your circumstances. Basically, there are four choices of rail material: brass, nickel silver, aluminum, and stainless steel.

Brass costs less than nickel silver but more than aluminum. It is not the best material, but it is, in my opinion, a reasonable choice. It is easy to work with and solders well. It does, though, require frequent cleaning if your trains are track powered.

Nickel silver is harder to work with. It is tougher than brass and more difficult to solder. It requires less frequent cleaning than brass but still requires occasional cleaning.

Aluminum is the least expensive material. It is also the softest of the four metals and can't be soldered. A sound mechanical/electrical connection is required for electric operation, which can be troublesome with aluminum rail. My advice is to avoid aluminum track.

Stainless steel is the most expensive of the rail materials. It is very hard, difficult to cut, and nearly impossible to solder. Some claim that no cleaning is required, but most track still needs an occasional cleaning to remove sediment. If stainless-steel flextrack is used, it is mandatory that a rail bender be used and that the rails be bent to the exact curvature. Clamp-on rail joiners should be used to secure the track since it can't be soldered. If you can overcome these difficulties, stainless steel is a good choice for track-powered railroads.

Selecting your track

The next thing to know about rail is its "code," which refers to the height of the rail. Code is nothing more than the height of the rail, measured in thousandths of an inch. Rail on LGB track is code 332, or .332" high (the standard for most manufacturers of large-scale equipment). Also available are smaller rails in codes 250 and 215.

Why code 250 or 215? If scale is important to you, and you look at code 332 track from a low angle or scale eye level, you will see that the rail is very tall—much taller than true scale. When codes 250 or 215 are viewed from the same angle, they appear more correctly

Code 332 rail is much taller than scale, and the bolts and brackets are European. However, this track is very robust and will take a lot of abuse. On the author's line, 90 percent of the track is code 332 and 10 percent is code 250.

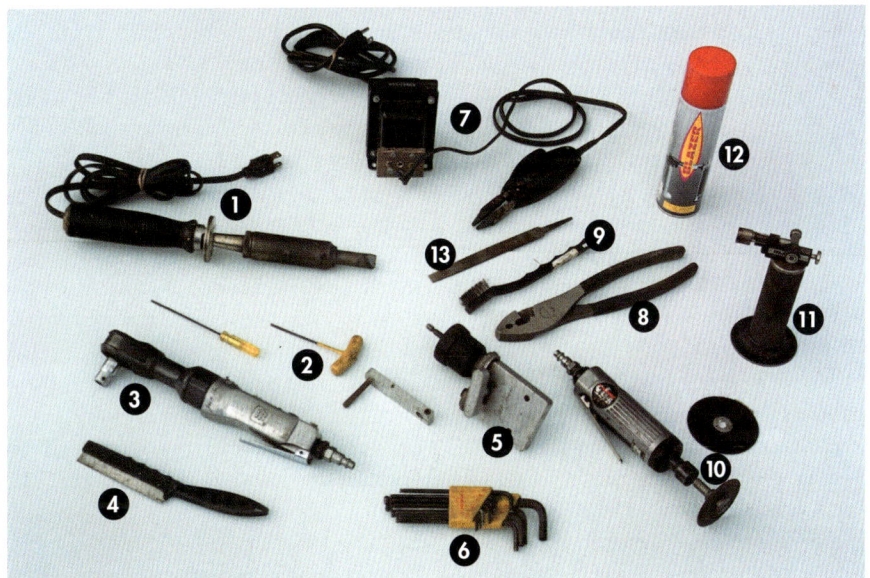

These are the basic tools for trackwork. 1. 175-watt soldering iron. 2. Allen wrenches with screwdriver handle and T-handle. 3. Air ratchet. 4. Atlas Super Saw. 5. Rail bender. 6. Allen wrench set. 7. Resistance soldering unit. 8. Pliers. 9. Stainless-steel wire brush. 10. Die grinder with extra cutting wheel. 11. Micro torch. 12. Butane gas.

proportioned. Personally, I like a scale look whenever possible.

The rails on LGB track are supported by plastic ties that are replicas of European sleepers (ties). In Europe, clamps and bolts are used to hold the rail in place. American rails are held down by smaller spike heads. This presents a problem in some garden railroads, especially those with limited or difficult access. Sometimes it's necessary to step on the track. Scale track does not handle foot traffic well. Due to the scale-size spike heads (represented by fragile plastic nubs), ties are easily stripped away from the rail when stepped on, creating serious maintenance problems.

LGB track is more robust and forgiving when abused. I personally recommend LGB flextrack for general-purpose garden-railroad use. It is the easiest to work with, is strong, and has proven reliable.

If you prefer a more scale appearance, code 250 rail could be used in areas that are not subject to abuse. The two different rail sizes can be joined together. Another trick with code 332 rail is to build the ballast up a little higher, over the tops of the ties, to make the rail look lower and to hide the European-style clamps and bolts.

In this chapter, I will be discussing the use of LGB flextrack. I recommend it because it allows you to form your

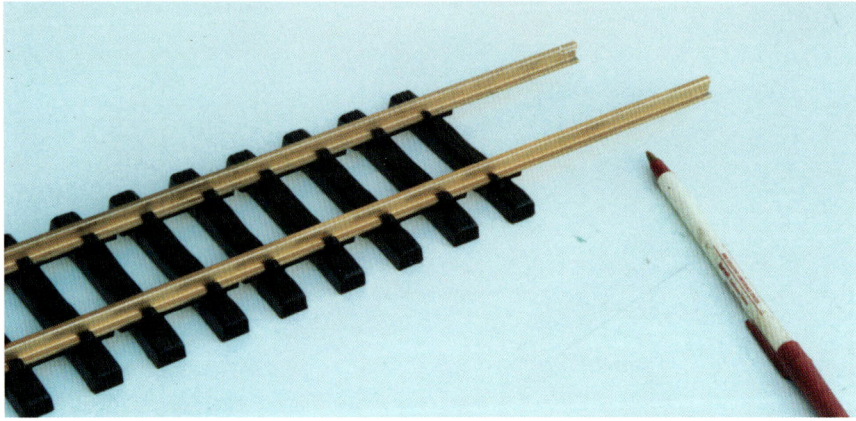

The rail on the inside of a curve is longer. Cut it off even with the outside rail.

railroad exactly to the terrain. You are not limited by fixed curves or lengths. Once you understand a few basic things about flextrack, you will enjoy working with it.

Assembling and bending track

There are three components to flextrack: rail, ties, and rail joiners. Assembly is easy. If you are making a straight section, just slide on the ties and rail joiners and connect it to the next piece. (If you are assembling several sections of flextrack in advance, use a rubber band wrapped around the rail ends to keep the ties from slipping off while you handle the track.) I cut the tabs off the LGB rail joiners to allow sliding the ties closer together at the joints.

Regarding curved track, remember that any train will work best on wide-radius curves. There will be less drag on the train, and it will have a more realistic appearance. All curves should be as broad as space permits. If you are making a curved section, you may have to use a rail bender to form the rail to the desired curve. Never bend flextrack over your knee or around an object—this will only kink it.

The rail bender consists of three rollers, one of which is adjustable. By tightening the adjustable roller, you apply a force to the rail in such a way that it will bend between the other two rollers. As you turn the crank, the rail passes through the rollers and is formed to shape. How much pressure you apply is a matter of trial and error. It seems that each rail bends a little differently than the next.

The best way to start is by increasing the pressure a little at a time until the

rail assumes the proper shape. If you bend it too far, you can put the rail through the bender backward to straighten it a little.

A rail bender should always be used for curved rail to be installed on a bridge or trestle or leading into a turnout. This eliminates the natural spring in the rail and ensures that it will not try to straighten out and knock the trestle or switch out of alignment.

It may be necessary to cut off some rail ends when using a rail bender because most benders do not form the last 1" of rail. If the curve is sharp, the ends must be cut off; if the curve is very gradual, this may not be necessary.

Soldered track

I prefer not to use a rail bender where the track is laid on the ground (as opposed to being on a bridge or trestle). Instead, I solder the track.

First, assemble the flextrack sections. Each section is about five feet long. Next, solder two sections together. You'll notice that the track will become more flexible as its length increases. Solder together as many pairs of sections as needed to cover the line. Next, take one of these double sections and lay it down where it will be installed, gently helping it conform to the roadbed. You will notice that the inside rail will be longer than the outside. Cut it so it's even with the outside rail. If your curve is a tight one, you may have to hold the rail in place, then mark it where it is to be cut. By following this procedure, you are letting the track lay down naturally. After trimming the first section of track, do the same for the next.

The next step is to solder the two double sections together. What holds the track in shape is that the inside rail has been cut to length and that each section is soldered to the next, creating a continuous, integrated track. The ballast, applied later, will also help hold the track in shape. The reason I like this method is that, when done correctly, you can actually form a smoother curve. Here's a simple rule: If the curve is sharp enough to need a rail bender, maybe you should be using sectional track. (The exceptions are trestles, bridges, and yard leads.)

Adjustments to the line

Once the track is laid on your subroadbed and soldered, it's time to level and ballast it.

Using a material scoop, pour ballast over the track and brush it in with a whisk broom or fox tail. Grade stakes are used here to ensure that the track is on grade. Use a torpedo level to level the track from side to side.

When using this method, you may occasionally run into a section of track that cannot be leveled from side to side with ballast. One side or the other seems to spring up. This is not a major problem—one rail or the other is simply too long. To correct this, cut through the high rail, remove a small amount of it, then rejoin the ends with a rail joiner. It may take one or two cuts to remove just the right amount of rail. Once the rail is level, solder the track back together. This same method can be used to superelevate track.

Soldering track

When I first became interested in garden railroading, I read all the articles I could find on trackwork. I discovered there was much controversy about soldering track. One of my biggest mistakes was not soldering my track when it was new. I strongly recommend soldering the track together, except at turnouts. Soldered rail joints eliminate electrical problems and form a strong mechanical joint. I solder track even if the railroad is going to be battery- or steam-powered.

The arguments against soldering are weak at best. One is that you need expansion joints. This is untrue. Yes, if

4

you have non-soldered joints you will see a gap open up when the temperature changes, but have you ever seen that gap close back up? Expansion and contraction of the track is handled by the roadbed. On a hot day, the track will widen at the curves. On a cold day, you may have a 10-foot radius, and on a hot day it might be 10'-1". This is why you should never anchor the track—it should be free to float in the ballast.

The other argument, which has some validity, concerns the option to change the track plan later. Still, this does not present a problem. You simply cut the track to remove it and re-solder it where needed. The reliability of soldered joints is worth the extra effort this may take.

I do not solder rail joiners at turnouts. Instead, I secure the ends with rail clamps, such as those manufactured by Richard Hillman. I have found that the majority of track plan changes are made at turnouts.

Here is the method I use to solder flextrack. I use 60/40 rosin core, wire-type solder. With brand-new flextrack, the rosin in the solder will provide enough flux. If the track is tarnished, it will be necessary to use additional soldering flux. I use a liquid-acid type flux. (Paste flux is very messy when used in the garden—everything sticks to it—but it can be used if you are doing penance.) The function of flux is to clean the metal. You may see a warning that says acid flux should not be used on electrical connections. This does not apply to track. We are actually making a structural connection.

If you are trying to solder old track that has turned black, you will have to clean it first. I start with copper-pot cleaner, then finish with flux. Once the rails have been prepared, slip on a rail joiner. If you are using acid flux, squirt a little into the joint. You are now ready to apply the heat.

There are several tools that can be used to solder track: a resistance-soldering unit; a large (175-200 watt) electric soldering iron with a chisel tip; or a micro torch. I have used all three and have found the micro torch the best all-around tool. The key to soldering is to get the work hot enough to melt the solder into the work.

Soldering tools. Top row: mini torch; 60/40 rosin-core solder; and liquid flux. Bottom row: heavy-duty pliers to align rails while the solder is hot; a wire brush for cleaning rail ends; and an Atlas Super Saw to cut the rails.

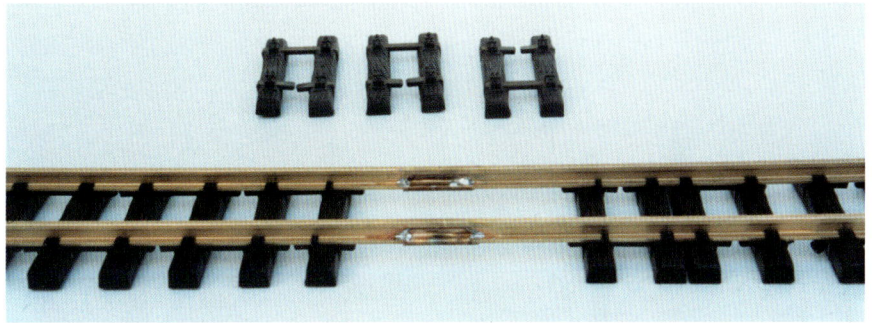

Here, two sections of flextrack have been soldered. Note that the solder has been drawn into the rail joiner at each end. To keep from melting the ties, cut the tie strips into pairs and remove the web on the ends. Slide the ties out of the way (see right side). When the joint is cool, slide the ties back into place.

Start heating the joint by passing the flame over it. This takes some practice. Don't hold the flame too close to the work. The blue tip of the flame should be about ⅛" to ¼" from the work. A little experimenting will teach you what the proper distance should be.

When the rail joiner starts to turn color, this means it is coming up to temperature. Start applying solder at one end of the rail joiner on the opposite side of the rail from where the flame is being applied. Touch the solder to the end of the rail joiner and let the heat pull it into the joint. The flame should never actually touch the solder. Once solder is pulled into one end of the joiner, do the same at the other end. Then apply the heat to the other side of the rail and repeat the process. If done properly, the solder will be very shiny and will flow evenly.

Take a large pair of pliers and grip the rails where they join. This will bring the rail heads into alignment, and the pliers will act as a heat sink to help cool the joint. Let the joint cool until solid before releasing the pliers. Wash the joint off with water to remove the flux.

If done properly, there shouldn't be any beads of solder on the joiners and the surface should be relatively smooth.

If you become proficient at soldering, you will be able to bond a joint without melting the plastic ties. The trick is to get in, get the metal hot enough to melt the solder, then get out.

Here is a trick that can help you until this skill is learned. Before installing the rail joiner, cut the webbing that connects the ties so you have three loose pairs of ties on either side of the joint (see the photo above). Remove the web completely from the ends of each pair. This will allow you to slide the ties safely away from the flame. When cool, slide them back into place.

Dealing with dilemmas

Derailments seem to be part of our hobby. There isn't a railroad anywhere that hasn't had one. However, they don't have to be an everyday occurrence. This chapter will address ways to troubleshoot your line if derailments are a continual problem.

An unfortunate occurrence on the author's railroad. With proper precautions, situations of this nature can be avoided.

Garden railroads are unique in model railroading. If left unattended for even a short time, things change. Leaves, small rocks, and other debris fall on the track and foul it. The first order of business in preventing derailments is to walk the line prior to running trains. I often find a variety of junk that falls on my own line—everything from pine needles to rocks. But derailments caused by natural disasters don't count. Here I will discuss those caused by mechanical faults and look at solutions.

If you suffer from chronic derailments, you must first determine if the cause is a defect in the rolling stock or a problem with the track. This is usually easy to figure out. If derailments always occur at the same location, but with different cars, the problem is most likely the track. On the other hand, if it's the same car that comes off the track all the time, it is most likely that car. Sometimes it's a combination of the two. In any case, troubleshooting is a process of elimination. Always check the most obvious first.

Wheels out of gauge

Out-of-gauge wheels (**fig. 1**) will most often cause derailments on turnouts. If the gauge is too wide, the wheels will roll up over the frog or the points. If too narrow, the wheels will ride up over the guard rails. In either case, the fix is to correct the gauge. Most wheels can be adjusted by pulling them apart, then pressing them back into proper gauge. A wheel gauge is needed to do this. If you do not have a wheel gauge, get one. Improper gauge can also cause derailments on curves, as the wheels may tend to ride up over the rails.

Rails out of gauge

Out-of-gauge rails can cause some weird problems. I had stretch of LGB flextrack on a curved grade. The train had problems climbing the grade with even a modest string of cars. In earlier times, it could easily pull more cars up the same grade. After close inspection, I noticed that several ties were broken or missing. After installing new ties where needed, I was able to run longer trains again. The out-of-gauge track (in this case, too tight) was acting like a brake against the wheel flanges (**fig. 2**).

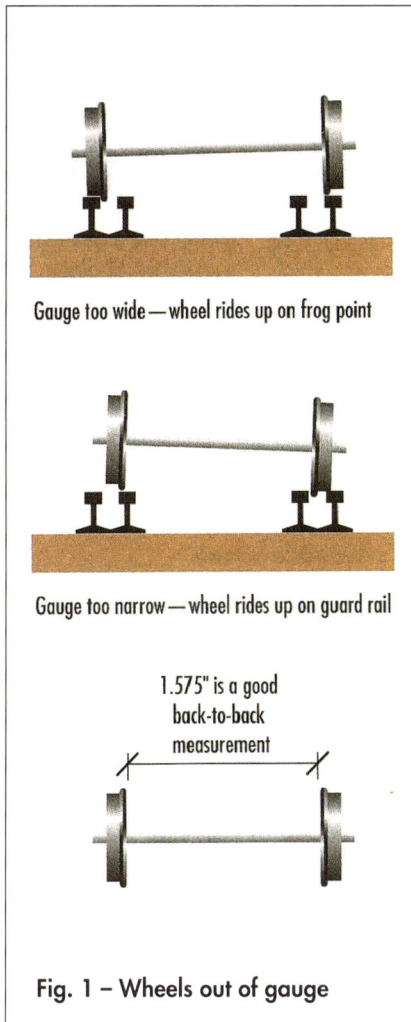

Gauge too wide—wheel rides up on frog point

Gauge too narrow—wheel rides up on guard rail

1.575" is a good back-to-back measurement

Fig. 1 – Wheels out of gauge

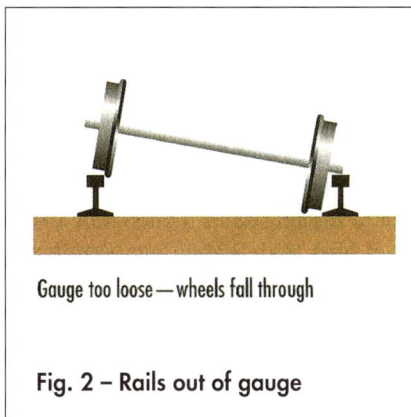

Gauge too loose—wheels fall through

Fig. 2 – Rails out of gauge

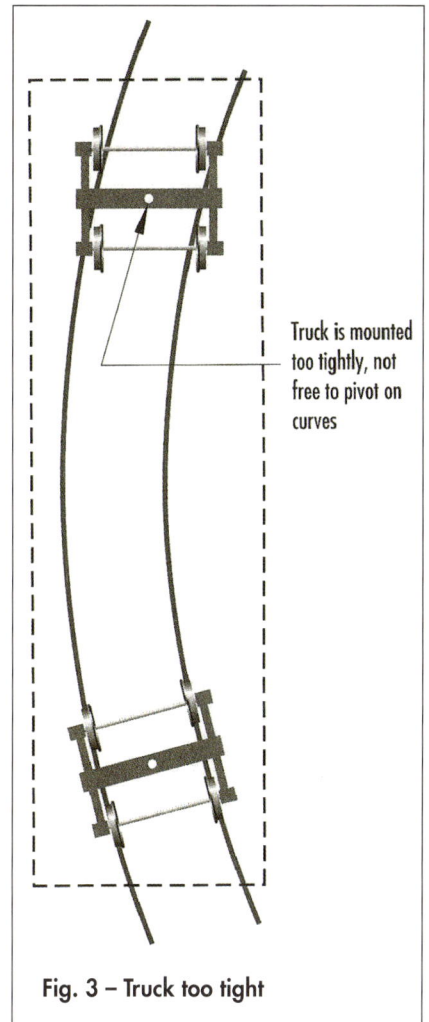

Truck is mounted too tightly, not free to pivot on curves

Fig. 3 – Truck too tight

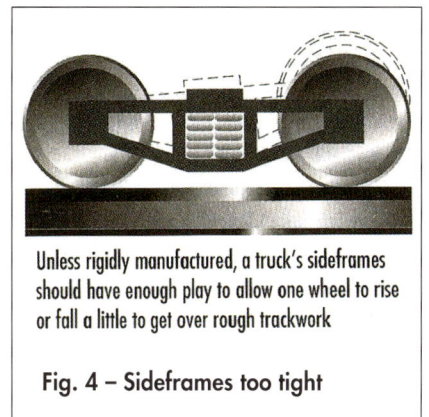

Unless rigidly manufactured, a truck's sideframes should have enough play to allow one wheel to rise or fall a little to get over rough trackwork

Fig. 4 – Sideframes too tight

Trucks too tight and do not pivot freely

A truck that does not turn freely will cause derailments, especially when going around curves (**fig. 3**). Trucks should pivot freely. To correct this, loosen the pivot point (the center mounting screw). It may be necessary to place a drop of Loc-Tite on the screw's threads to keep the screw from backing out. (Don't get glue on the

truck itself. You will have a worse problem if you do.)

A related problem could be that a truck's sideframes are too tight. Check the motion of the sideframes. On certain brands, such as LGB, the sideframe should be flexible enough to allow all four wheels to touch the rails, or for a wheel to lift slightly to get over rough trackwork (**fig. 4**). Sometimes, if the truck's sideframes are too tight, one

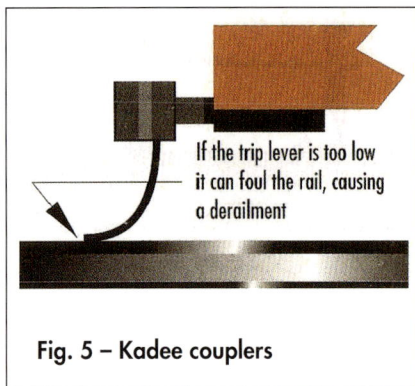

If the trip lever is too low it can foul the rail, causing a derailment

Fig. 5 – Kadee couplers

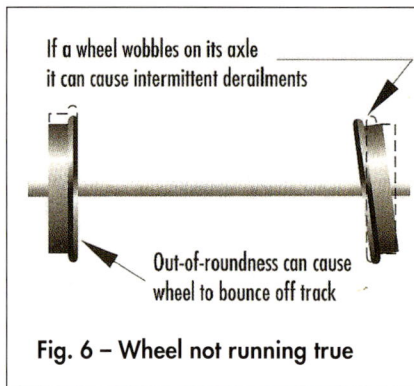

If a wheel wobbles on its axle it can cause intermittent derailments

Out-of-roundness can cause wheel to bounce off track

Fig. 6 – Wheel not running true

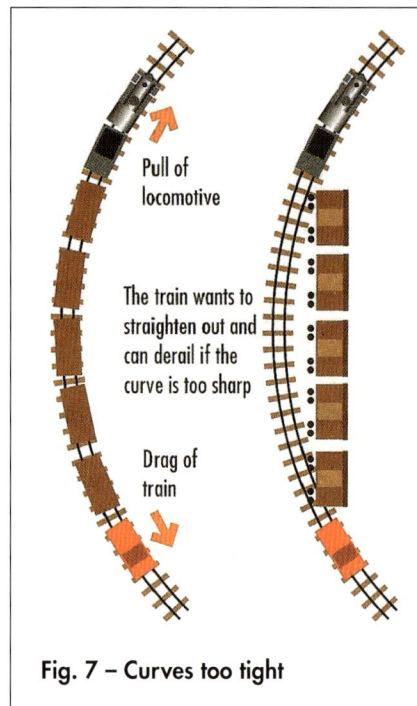

Pull of locomotive

The train wants to straighten out and can derail if the curve is too sharp

Drag of train

Fig. 7 – Curves too tight

wheel may be stuck in an up position, not touching the track. This is easy to correct. Just rotate the sideframe until the wheels sit on the track correctly.

Another related problem is that sometimes, especially on kitbashed rolling stock, the truck hangs up on something protruding from the car. I once knew of a stock diesel locomotive that kept coming off the track on a certain curve. We examined the track and could find nothing wrong. It turned out that the engine's truck hung up on a molded band around an air tank. Once the band was trimmed, it ran fine.

An object protruding from the car or locomotive is hitting something

The train is running fine, then all of a sudden it comes to an abrupt halt, or you hear a "crunch" or "clunk."

This often happens after you have kitbashed something and not realized that a new part, such as a step or other protruding object, sticks out too far. End steps that are low can hit the track, grade-crossing planks, or turnout parts; or marker lights can hit the sides of a tunnel or other structure, causing the car to tip over. These, of course, are easy to correct. It is best to test-run new equipment before you have visitors over.

Kadee couplers

If the trip lever on a Kadee coupler at the head end of a car hangs too low, it will catch on things like whistle-and-bell track magnets, track contacts for block controls, and turnout parts (**fig. 5**). This became such a problem on my line that I cut all the trip levers off and now use a homemade tool to open the couplers. The trip levers should be set to Kadee specifications as shown in their instruction sheets.

A similar thing can happen with LGB-style hook-and-loop couplers if the hook spring is weakened. The hook can hang down, looking for something to snag. The fix is to replace the plastic spring (LGB part no. 64409).

Wheels out of round or not true

I had a car that derailed intermittently at turnouts, depending on which part of the wheel was on the rail as it went through the switch. Intermittent problems can be annoying because they never occur when you are looking. It turned out that a wheel was wobbling on its axle (**fig. 6**). It was not out of round, but it was not square with the axle. To check for this, turn the car upside down and spin the wheels to see if they run true.

Cars too light to hold the wheels down

This can be a problem on plastic flatcars and other small rolling stock. The best way to add weight to a car is to add metal wheels. These are solid metal (except for the axle insulator) and are much heavier than plastic wheels. A good investment, if you want to run longer trains, is to purchase ball-bearing wheels. These wheels spin free of the axle and eliminate friction and drag.

Track not level side-to-side

This can be a bigger problem on curves, where a train is more likely to roll over. Track should be close to level from side-to-side, even on curves.

Another less obvious, but closely related, problem is soft ballast—ballast that does not sufficiently support the track, causing the track to sink when the engine runs over it. This is a bigger problem with locomotives that have higher centers of gravity, such as

steam-outline engines. The solution is to ballast the track with a more substantial material, such as gray fines.

Track is kinked or gaps are too wide at rail joints

This can cause a car to be thrown from the track. A kink (or dogleg) is difficult to repair (unless it is at the rail joiner). It is usually necessary to replace the offending section of track to eliminate a kink. If the kink is at a soldered rail joiner, you can usually fix it by heating the solder joint and realigning the rails by gripping them with a pair of pliers.

A curve is too sharp or poorly engineered

Sharp turns can cause derailments or rollovers on longer trains. When traveling through a sharp curve, the center cars in a long train can be pulled over by the tension caused by the pull of the locomotive and friction between the train and track (**fig. 7**). The solution is to use broader curves or run shorter trains.

Points not fully closed

Sometimes ballast or debris gets into switch points, holding them partially open. A close inspection before running will usually reveal this. Other times, even when the points are closed tightly, a car may derail when a wheel hits a point rail. Filing the points may help.

CHAPTER 6

Adding drama

This trestle followed the full-size practice of using different lengths of trestle-bent legs to cross this pre-existing rock valley.

A train crossing a body of water has a magical effect. Trestles and bridges can add an element of drama as trains traverse a narrow structure several feet above the ground. In this chapter, I'll show you some useful tools and methods I have used to make bridges and trestles with character.

That something as big and heavy as a train can safely travel high over water or across a ravine on a trestle, rather than having to go around these obstacles, is a civil-engineering wonder. A tall trestle gives a scene a sense of drama, and even a low trestle will add realism to the garden railroad. Many wooden trestles still exist on full-size railroads, although others are in ruins. A nicely done trestle in a garden railroad is guaranteed to be a primary point of interest.

Making a trestle look right takes some planning. It should blend into the scenery. Even though a trestle is man-made, it should look like it belongs where it is. If you study full-size railroads, you will notice that trestles are used to cross gaps, usually over dry land, where a fill is impractical. Trestles are also used in mountainous areas, where they are used to connect lines between ledges along hillsides. When laying out your railroad, plan for a trestle by creating a low area that will need to be bridged.

The difference between a bridge and trestle, for the purpose of this chapter, is that a bridge is basically a beam that has its own support system, such as a truss, built into it. It can span a long distance without additional support. A trestle is a series of short bridges supported by vertical members called bents. Spans between bents can vary anywhere from about eight to 20 feet. Trestles can be curved, and there is no limit to their length.

Knowing when to use a bridge and when to use a trestle will help make your railroad more realistic. In general, trestles are used whenever possible because of their lower construction costs. A trestle can be used in almost any application and be prototypically correct. A bridge should be used more conservatively. Bridges are commonly used for crossing water, since fewer vertical supports are needed. The bridge itself is always straight, although the track across it may be curved. A series of bridges can be used to span a large gap, with a minimal amount of vertical support.

Trestle construction

Trestles appear to be complex structures. They are, however, easier to build than you might think. The key to trestle construction is to take the project step by step. First, you need to make the trestle bents, the main vertical members of the structure. These can be prefabricated in the workshop.

I like to make my bents in a four-legged configuration, with the outside legs angled outward at about 12 degrees. This is how real trestle bents are built, and it makes the trestle look taller and adds stability. I like to use timbers that are slightly under scale to make the finished trestle look more spindly. For the main timbers, I use ½"-square stock. For stringers (the beams that connect the bents at the top and upon which the track is laid) I also use ½"-square lumber, although you could use wood up to ⅝" square. For braces (both horizontal and diagonal), I use ¼" x ⅜" strips. These sizes are not intended to be exactly to scale, but they combine good appearance and reasonable strength.

You can cut your own timbers on a table saw. Redwood is the material of choice. Although it has a natural resistance to rotting, you should still treat the parts that will be underground with a wood preservative.

The first step in making the bents is to draw a plan like that shown in the sidebar on page 63, then make a construction jig. While the bent is still in the jig, you can install all of the cross braces on one side. Remove the bent from the jig to install the remaining braces. It's a good idea to both glue and nail the braces in place. Titebond II is a waterproof wood glue that works well for this.

Depending on the application, you can make the bents different heights. I call them sizes one, two, and three, depending on how many horizontal cross-brace sections each has. If in doubt, make the bents longer than necessary. You can always cut them to size on-site.

If you are installing a straight trestle in dirt, you can prefabricate the whole structure on the workbench. However, I like to build mountainous scenery, and I will often install a trestle across rocky terrain, both on a curve and on an incline, which makes installation an interesting challenge.

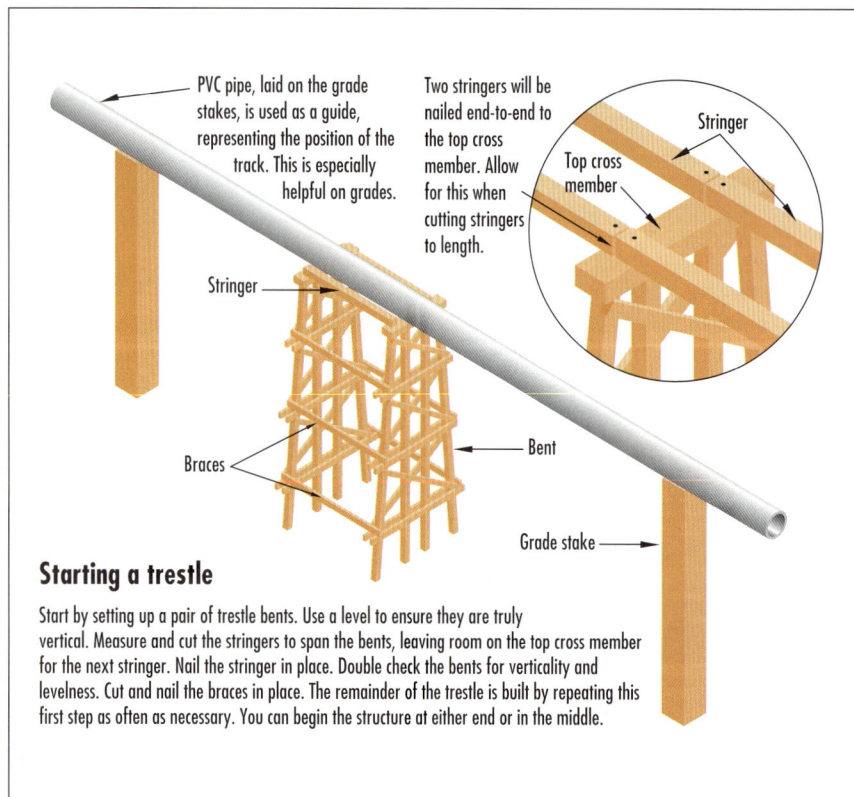

PVC pipe, laid on the grade stakes, is used as a guide, representing the position of the track. This is especially helpful on grades.

Two stringers will be nailed end-to-end to the top cross member. Allow for this when cutting stringers to length.

Stringer

Top cross member

Stringer

Braces

Bent

Grade stake

Starting a trestle

Start by setting up a pair of trestle bents. Use a level to ensure they are truly vertical. Measure and cut the stringers to span the bents, leaving room on the top cross member for the next stringer. Nail the stringer in place. Double check the bents for verticality and levelness. Cut and nail the braces in place. The remainder of the trestle is built by repeating this first step as often as necessary. You can begin the structure at either end or in the middle.

This is the type of installation that will be discussed here.

If you refer to Chapter 1, you will see how to set up grade stakes. I have modified that system a bit, and I now simulate the track by using PVC pipe fastened to the tops of the grade stakes with drywall screws. This system works especially well for trestle installation. The bents can be installed against the bottom of the pipe, thus ensuring that the trestle is at the proper grade. It is not important for the bents to be installed at exactly the right height at first pass—their exact positions can be adjusted in the final stages of trestle installation.

Working on a curve is tricky, but it is easier if you follow prototype practice. The first step is to set up the first bent, followed by the second. You can use twist-ties to hold the bents in position under the PVC pipe. Using a level, set the bents upright and level, then measure them for the stringer length. Measure from the center of the top cross member to the center of the next top cross member. The inside stringer on a curved trestle will be shorter. Next, install the side braces. Double-check the bents to ensure they are plumb, then measure and cut the braces. Nail the braces in place. You now have a short bridge. The rest of the installation is merely a repetition of this process.

When working on rocky terrain, you will have to cut each leg of the bent to the correct length. (An easier way is to install the bents in soil and add the rocks later.) I think a trestle built over rock, with legs of different lengths, looks very realistic. Use mortar to fill any gaps, since it is difficult to get the leg height exactly right. The mortar can be colored to blend with the rocks. In some cases, you can use wooden shims to make up small differences.

In actual practice, different methods were used to support trestle bents. Sometimes the legs were just driven into the ground. These are called pile trestles. Other trestles had the bottoms of the bent legs resting on concrete piers or cut-stone footings. These are known as frame trestles.

With the information outlined here and in the sidebars, you should be able to construct trestles of any size to fit your garden railway.

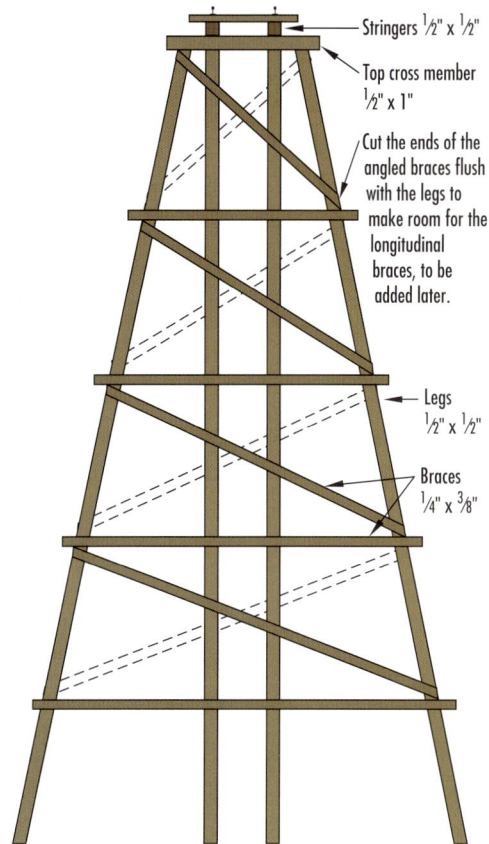

Stringers ½" x ½"

Top cross member ½" x 1"

Cut the ends of the angled braces flush with the legs to make room for the longitudinal braces, to be added later.

Legs ½" x ½"

Braces ¼" x ⅜"

Trestle bent

This trestle bent is suitable for garden-railroad use. Enlarge it 550% for large scale. The timbers can be smaller or larger, as you like. An enlarged drawing can be used to make an assembly jig, as outlined below.

All of the solid-colored components can be added while the bent is in the jig. The reverse-side braces (dotted) must be added when the bent is removed.

Building and using a jig

A jig to assemble the bents will ensure that they are uniform and true. An easy way to make one is to enlarge your plan to full size, then simply lay things out on top of the drawing, using it as your guide.

Another method is to glue the full-size drawing to a piece of hardboard or particle board. Cut the legs to size and place them on the drawing. Nail small pieces of wood as guides next to the legs. These will allow you to place the next set of parts in the jig in exactly the same position.

Once the legs are in position, nail the cross braces in place on one side of the bent, using the drawing as a guide. Once you have one side nailed, remove the bent from the jig, then nail on the backside braces.

I leave the top cross member off until all of the other cross members are in place. Then, I use a sander to true up the tops of the legs, after which I nail the ½" x 1" top cross member in place. This odd size ensures an adequate nailing surface for installing the stringers later on.

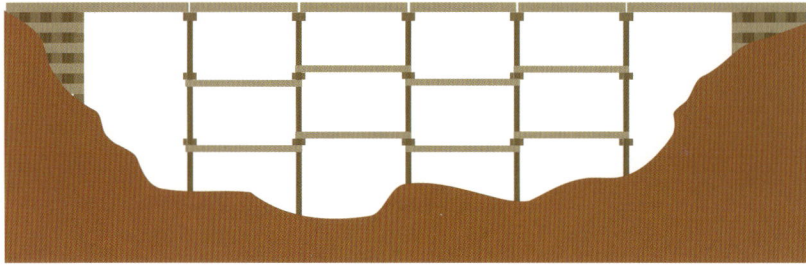

Trestle bracing

Longitudinal trestle braces are often staggered. They do not have to be perfectly aligned for strength. In looking at photos of trestles, you will see that many were built to be strong, not pretty. You may even see braces that are crooked. In some cases, trestles were built with recycled materials.

X-bracing can be added if you wish. I leave it out in most cases because it tends to make the structure look very "busy." Full-size trestles were built both with and without X-bracing.

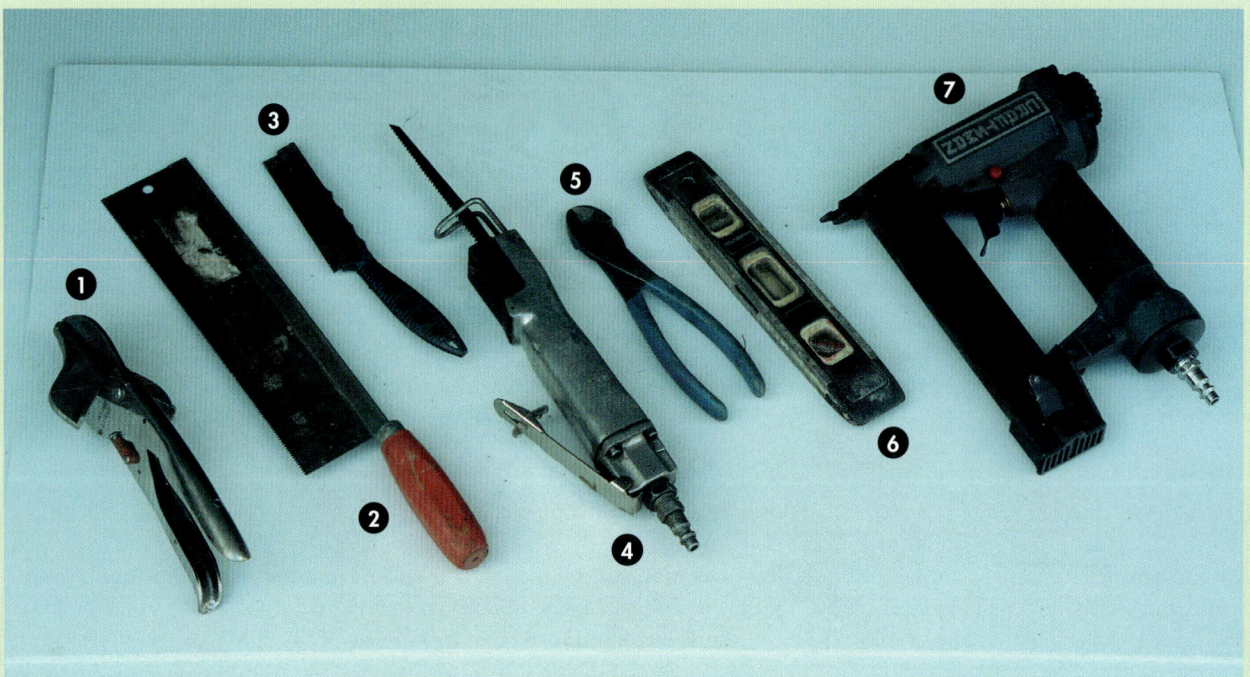

Tools

There are a few tools that are a must for trestle construction. A brad gun (**7**) is the No. 1 labor-saving tool used in building trestles. I built one trestle without a brad gun, and it was a real project. I had to predrill each hole, then push a nail in with a pair of pliers. A hammer could not be used because it would knock the wood out of alignment.

With a brad gun, you place its tip where you want the brad, then pull the trigger. The brad is driven in instantly and cleanly, and it does not stress the structure. With a little practice, you become very proficient. Both electric and air-operated brad guns are available.

A razor saw (**3**) is a fine-tooth handsaw for making very fine cuts in wood. A dovetail saw (**2**) is similar, but a little heavier. A power saber saw (not shown) also works well. My favorite tool is an air-operated fender saw (**4**). In real life, this is used to cut sheet metal. It is air operated, easy to handle, and resembles a Sawzall in miniature. Before using one for our purposes, you must replace the original metal-cutting blade with one for wood.

Another wood-cutting device is a scissors-type cutter (**1**), which works well for cutting braces. Its cut is not as smooth as a saw, but it is quicker. A pair of side cutters (**5**) is also good to have on hand. This can be used to remove misfired brads or an entire brace. A small level (**6**) is used to position the bents. You will need one that will read in the vertical axis as well as the horizontal.

▲ A Swiss-style passenger train crosses the new resin-and-concrete viaduct on Dick Robertshaw's line.

Stone viaducts

Stonework viaducts and bridges have always impressed me, especially those on Swiss railways. In building a couple of Swiss-style garden railroads, I was faced with the challenge of making models of these. I haven't found any commercially available stone-arch viaducts that have the Swiss look.

Since viaducts would inevitably be on or near a pathway (for ease of maintenance), I wanted to make sure that whatever method I used, the resulting product would be nearly indestructible. After much contemplation, I came up with a system I like. It has the detail and strength of cast concrete, but is relatively quick to make. This method uses hollow cast-resin piers and arches, which are filled with mortar as they are erected.

To start, I made patterns of the viaduct that I wanted. I found a drawing in a book and had it enlarged to the size I wanted, then used it as my plan. I divided the structure into three parts: the arched section, the pier's side walls, and the inside walls. (The pier's inside wall also doubles as the inside of the arch; more on that later.) The arched side walls required the most thought, since the ends would have to interlock like tongues and grooves. The idea was that the arch walls can interlock in succession to make a continuous wall as long as desired. A cardboard test template was useful in working out the challenge of matching them up.

Master patterns and casting

Master parts can be made using several techniques. They could be made of wood, real stone, carved extruded foam, or a combination of all three. I decided to use stones that I bought at a doll-house store. These were not real stones, but castings of flat stones to be used in a wall or pathway for a dollhouse. They were made of a material that could be cut and trimmed with scissors.

I cut several stones into the shapes and sizes I needed. After making about 20 stones, I made a mold of them and then cast my own stones. Once I had a supply of cast stones, it was just a matter of gluing them to my pattern. When the masters were done, I made an RTV rubber mold of each part. (Casting resin and RTV mold rubber are available from Micro-Mark and other sources.)

At this point, I had three molds: One to make the right and left sides of the arch, one to make the right and left sides of the pier, and one to make the inside walls. Cleats, similar to I-beams, were needed to hold the structure together when completed, and these I also cast in resin in an RTV mold. See the photo on page 66.

The next step is to cast a supply of parts. This goes quickly. The casting resin cures enough in about five minutes for the part to be removed from the mold. All the parts, except for the inside of the arch, are straightforward.

To make the inside arch, I made a casting in the inside-wall mold, but pulled it from the mold early while it was still soft and easily bent. The soft wall was laid over a mandrel shaped to match the arch, then left to harden. This takes just a few minutes, so the work must be done quickly.

All parts, except the inside wall of the arch, must have cleats molded into them, so I made up a supply before casting the other pieces. When I pour the resin into the mold, I place a cleat into the mold as well. Half the cleat will be embedded in the resin; the other half protrudes. When the casting has cured, the cleat will become an integral

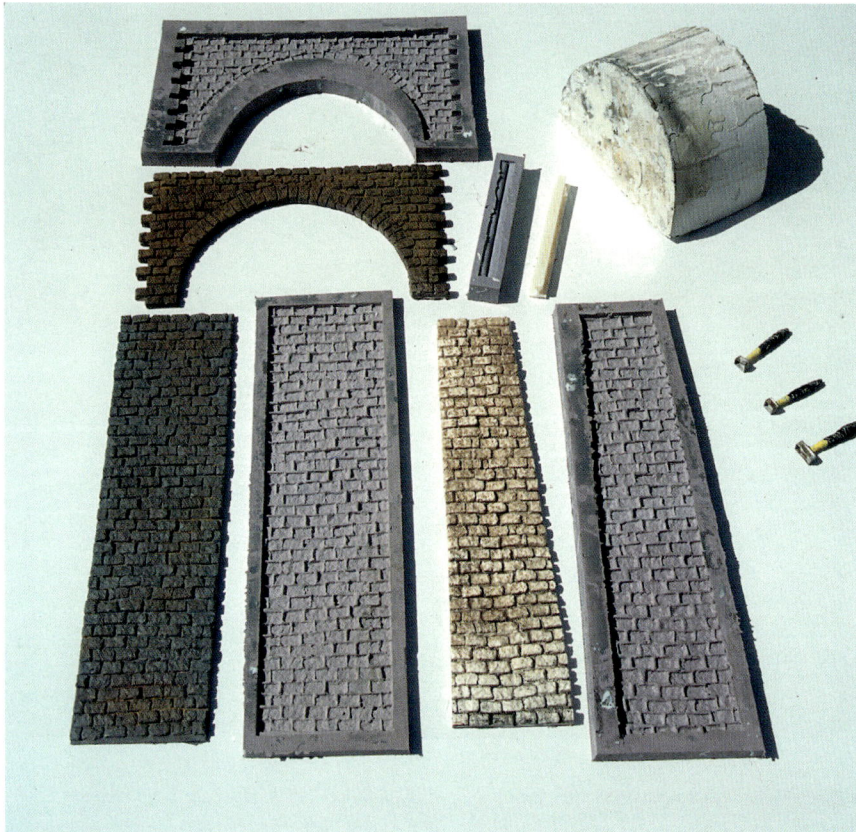

▲ At upper left is the mold for the arch side walls; below it is the actual part. At lower left is the inside pier wall, with its mold to its right. This mold is also used to make the inner wall of the arch. To the right of the inner wall mold is the pier side wall. To the right of the arch is the cleat mold and a finished cleat. At far right are homemade "cookie cutters," used for making stone patterns in concrete structures. At upper right is the shaping block for the inside arch.

part of it. These cleats will hold the parts together later, and interlock with the cement.

Assembly

I use cyanoacrylate adhesive (CA) to temporarily hold the parts together. Two assemblies are made. The first is the pier, made from two inside walls and two side walls. The other is the arch, made from two arch side pieces and an inside arch formed to fit.

After I have enough piers and arches assembled, I am ready to build the viaduct. I start by digging a 4" to 5" trench where the piers will go. I then set up the first pier and drive a piece of rebar into the ground, through the middle of the pier, with about 2" of the rebar protruding above the top of the pier. Next, I fill the pier with mortar,

▼ Several sections of the viaduct have been fitted loosely together at right. A trench in which the piers will sit will be dug under the PVC pipe. This viaduct is on a 2.5 percent grade, so the pipe helps keep the structure aligned to the grade as well as in line. To make the grade, the arches are stepped up or down one notch at each joint. Note the pile of viaduct parts at left.

allowing it to ooze out of the bottom to form a footing around the base.

The second pier is set up the same way. I use the arch to determine the spacing between the piers. I fill the second pier mold with mortar, then place the first arch mold on the piers and fill the arch about halfway up with mortar. This holds the piers and arches in place, but allows for adjustments to be made for several minutes until the mortar sets. These steps are repeated until the viaduct is completely laid out. When filling the pier molds with mortar, I let the mortar that oozes from the bottom flow over to the next pier. This adds strength by giving the viaduct a continuous footing, which is covered by soil when finished.

The final step is to lay a piece of re-bar between the walls for the full length of the viaduct, then fill the rest of the structure with mortar. When done, the viaduct is strong enough to walk on.

The viaduct is now ready to paint. Since the surface is resin, a variety of techniques can be used. It can simply be spray-painted, or it could be stained with a wash of acrylic paints.

Curved viaducts

In full-size practice, curved viaducts are actually a series of short straight sections. Each arch section is straight. The curve is made at the piers, where the inside walls of the arches are shorter than the outside wall.

The same system discussed above can be used to make a curved viaduct, but the inside wall of each arch must be cut shorter; about ½" per side will work for a five-foot-radius turn. I cut the tongues off and butt the walls together. The side wall of the pier on the inside of the curve will be slightly wider than the arch wall where it meets the pier, but it is not that noticeable. The next time I do a curved viaduct, I plan to make a separate mold for an inside wall, to eliminate having to cut the walls.

There are always gaps between the segments. I use mortar to fill them and a sponge to shape, smooth, and clean up the mortar.

▲ This arch bridge is made entirely of concrete. The stonework was made using the pattern-making tools.

SECTION 3:
Concrete arch bridges

Sometimes I need a special single-arch bridge for a one-of-a-kind project, and a cast-concrete structure is often the best choice. To make the form, I first make a scale drawing, then enlarge it to full size on a copy machine. I then lay out the pattern on a piece of fiberboard (you can also use hardboard, such as Masonite). Walls are added to the form to define the basic shape of the bridge (see the drawing on page 68). I use extruded foam board for the walls, but you could also use hardboard. For the main arch, I use a combination of foam board (cut to shape) and styrene plastic. I make smaller arches out of solid foam.

When the form box is complete, I place rebar in it and fill the mold with

Pattern-making tools for imitating stonework

These tools are basically cookie cutters. They can be made of styrene plastic or metal, though metal works better.

Take a piece of thin brass and form a rectangular box the size of an individual stone. Solder this box to a brass baseplate, then solder a handle to the baseplate. Decide what size you want your blocks to be and make a tool for each size. You will need at least one full-size block, one half size, and a keystone block. An additional tool can be made to add lines or touch up mistakes. This can be just a piece of brass soldered to a handle.

To use this method on buildings, you could build special tools for making archways over doors and windows, or whatever other special shapes might be required. The possibilities are endless.

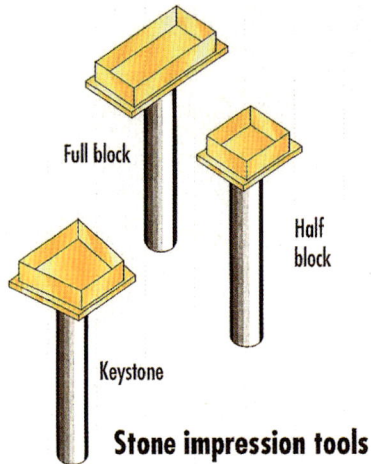

Full block

Half block

Keystone

Stone impression tools

mortar. Then I set the project aside for one week. It is important that the mortar be completely cured before trying to remove the bridge from the form. To remove the bridge, I break away the foam.

At this point, I have a concrete bridge with no texture. To add stone texture, I paint the surface with a thin coating of concrete adhesive. Then I spread a thin layer of gulapata (see the sidebar on page 82 in Chapter 8) over the entire bridge and trowel it smooth. Then, using several brass shaping tools that resemble cookie cutters, I lightly stamp the stone pattern into the surface. (The sidebar at left explains how to make these stone-forming tools).

You can use the same method to make stone retaining walls and buildings as well as bridges. The cookie-cutter pattern makers work best when the mortar is still wet, but has set for a few minutes. Once the mortar has set hard, this tool cannot be used.

Concrete

Styrofoam former

Styrene

Solid styrofoam block

Baseboard

Styrofoam form sides

Casting concrete bridges

Finished casting

An alternative method for imitation stone

If you can't work fast enough with mortar, try another cement mixture that I use: a mixture of one part Portland cement, two parts vermiculite, and three parts water. This material can be carved. I use it mainly for making simulated stone walls and other such items.

I apply this mixture to any surface that can take regular cement or mortar. I apply a coating, then wait one day before carving it. It will remain relatively soft and workable for about a week, after which time it hardens. The material works almost like putty. You can make impressions in it while it's wet. When it's partially cured, you can use a sharp object to cut or carve in lines. If a piece falls off, it can be reattached by wetting it and pushing it back into place (but only while it's still pliable, about one or two days old). It can be colored with concrete dye for several days after application. The material absorbs colors well.

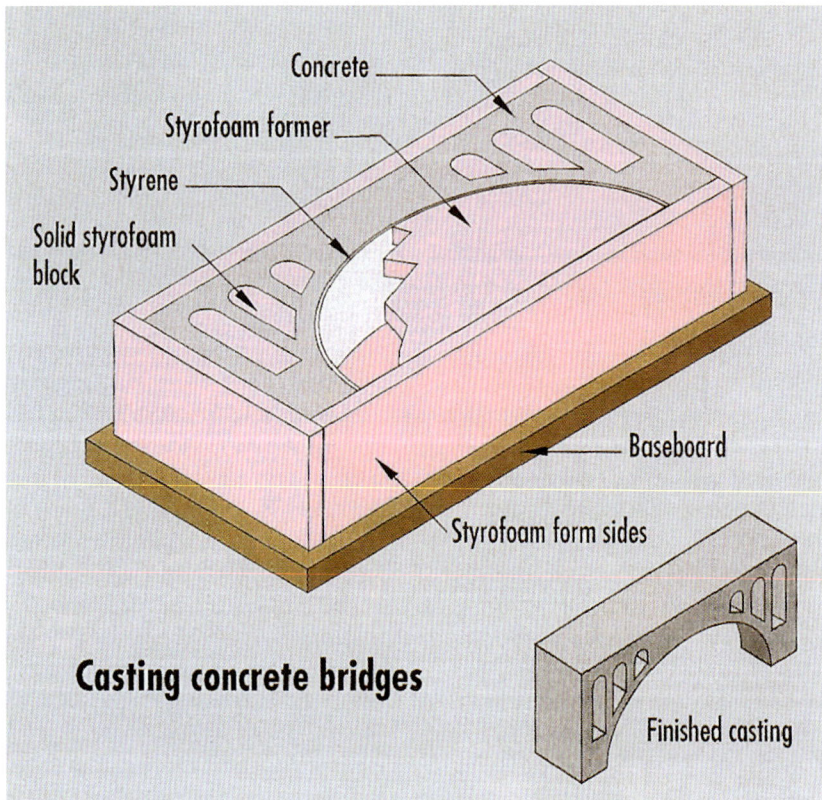

CHAPTER 7 **Structures**

A Chamaecyparis pisifera 'Plumosa Compressa' has been shaped into a formal "broom-style" tree. Planted next to this structure, it looks like an old oak tree.

Structures give your railroad a purpose and a sense of scale. They add color and life, and incorporating them into your garden can be as much fun as operating trains. I'll show you how to use structures in your garden railway, how to place them to look like a miniature town, and how to use plants and trees together successfully.

SECTION 1:
Landscaping with model structures

The placement of structures on your railroad should be done with the same thought and care that you invested in the rest of your railroad. It makes no sense to spend hours building and detailing model structures, then place them haphazardly on the ground. I attended a garden-railroad event some time ago. On the cover of the program was a photo of a beautiful building with surrounding details. Needless to say, I put that railroad on my "must see" list. After arriving, to my disappointment, I saw what did not show up in the picture. Structures were not level and were displayed in unnatural settings, almost like they were just set out on the ground. The buildings themselves were nicely done. If the builder had spent just a little more time in the placement of them, the total effect would have been stunning.

A garden railroad doesn't have to have structures in it, and I have seen some very nice lines that had just a few buildings. I happen to enjoy building structures, so I don't subscribe to the this practice.

Like plants, structures can be used as landscaping. There are many ways to use buildings to create special effects. Structures can lend scale to your work and can accent certain features. For example, a small Japanese maple by itself can get lost in a larger garden setting. But if you place a miniature building next to it, the maple is now accented. Structures can also add color to the garden, just as flowers do in full-size gardens.

Structures can add depth to your garden; they can lead the eye into the scene you are creating. In this chapter, rather than discussing the construction of structures, the emphasis will be on using them as part of your landscape and creating a vignette or a town.

Town planning

In designing your railroad, consider leaving open spaces to create the illusion of distance between towns. It is tempting to fill every space with a structure. You will be more satisfied if you place your buildings in groups or settlements, leaving open space in between. The illusion created is that of time and distance to be traveled by the train. I have done this on my railroad by designating certain areas as "no-build" zones.

The purpose of this chapter is to direct your thinking, rather than to give you a set of rules. If you are depicting a modern-era railroad, all you have to do is look around to see how structures are laid out. For earlier times, look at old photos. While studying old pictures, I

Helping root-bound plants

When you buy a plant, you'll sometimes find that it's been in the pot for a while (**photo A**). If the roots are tightly packed and growing in circles (known as "root-bound"), you'll need to comb the roots out to allow them to spread evenly. The tool shown in the bottom of **photo B** has a small hook that is used to gently break up the root ball and separate the tangled roots. If this is not done, the roots will continue to grow in circles. If the root ball is not too tightly packed, it only may be necessary to shake it a little to get the roots to spread out. Combing the roots (**photo C**) makes it much easier to plant in tight areas, such as between rocks.

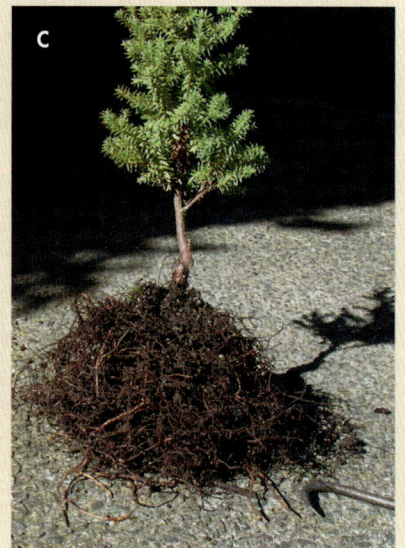

found it interesting to see the many ways towns were laid out. Buildings were sometimes built in a straight row. They often ran alongside the railroad. In early days, most towns sprang up along the tracks. In some cases, like in gold-rush-era Skagway, Alaska, or modern-day Oakland, California, the tracks ran right down the middle of the street.

Sometimes towns were built along a river or a stream bank. Sometimes they were built next to an industry; in the case of a company town, everything was next to or near the factory. Some small towns were built around a town square or a central park. In some cases, towns or homes had to be built on hillsides. As you can see, there are many ways to lay out a town.

Planting structures

Here are a few guidelines I follow in setting model structures into my railroad.

• Don't overwhelm the space. Almost anything can be reproduced in scale except space. With few exceptions, we are all working with limited spaces. I have found that when a structure goes into a given space, it will often dominate the area. For example, I have a pond that looks like a mountain lake, appearing large in photos where there are no scale references. I decided to add a small dock and a boathouse. As soon as I set them in place, the lake seemed to shrink. The boathouse gave scale to the scene and revealed that the pond was really not very big.

Two ways to deal with this phenomenon are to model small structures or work in a slightly smaller scale than the trains. I model all my structures in 1:24 scale, even though the trains are 1:20.3 scale. If I modeled structures in 1:20.3, I would not have room for them in my railroad (or I would have far fewer structures). As long as undersize structures are not displayed too close to the trains, they will work.

It is important not to mix scales in close proximity to each other. If I have a 1:24 structure, I would not display 1:20.3 scale (on the larger side) or 1:32 scale (on the smaller side) details next to it. This would draw attention to the difference. If you have virtually unlimited space, it is always better to build your structures in the same scale as the trains. Since I don't, I have forgiven myself for the different scales. I just try to keep everything in correct proportion to each other.

Be careful not to mix scale figures. Placing a 1:20.3 person next to a 1:24 door really draws attention to the difference. One cure for this is to make your doors 1:20.3 scale even though the rest of the building is 1:24. In studying old photos, I noticed that some doors were very tall, so a large door may not be out of character.

• Always level your structures to the ground. There is nothing more annoy-

Scale reference

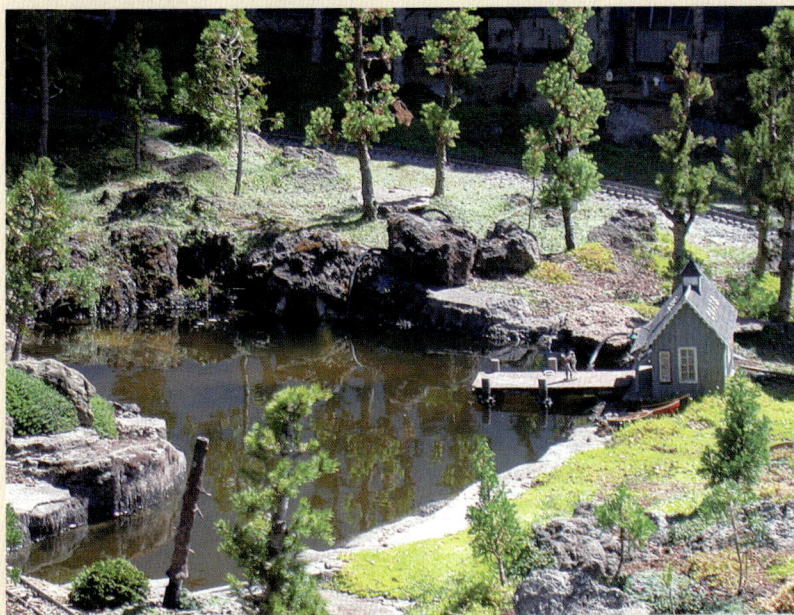

Without scale reference, this lake could be any size. Once you add a boathouse, dock, or railroad tracks, you introduce a scale reference. The mind will view the scene based on these reference points. In most cases, the natural landscape will look smaller with structures in place.

ing to me than seeing structures that are all askew. Even in a real-life ghost town, a structure that is leaning over and ready to collapse is usually level at the base. To keep structures level, I like to install a base or foundation.

• Use low-growing ground covers around structures. Irish and Scotch moss, creeping mint, and green carpet are good choices. Always select plants with small leaves for use around structures. Most plants have leaves that are much larger than true scale, so be selective about what you use. Avoid flowing ground covers around structures.

• Miniature trees and shrubs will make the scene come to life. Make sure you plant trees far enough away from buildings so that when they grow, they do not become a problem. Some

Several miniature plants, including dwarf boxwood and cotoneasters, have been used to blend the cottage into the scene. They soften the scene and give it a sense of life.

trees can be pruned from time to time to overcome this. Others grow too fast, so avoid them. The same is true of ground covers. Plants like blue star creeper can engulf a building in one growing season.

• Whenever space permits, a road and walkways should be added to each scene. With the exception of wilderness cabins, most buildings will have road access. You can add a road even if it does not connect to another scene. The idea is to suggest a connection to other structures or places. Roads also offer detailing opportunities. You can display model cars and trucks, or horse-drawn vehicles when depicting an older era.

Fog Harbor is a coastal town on the author's railroad. It was developed around the railroad, just as many real-life towns were. The main line runs in front of the lighthouse/train station and behind the commercial-row part of town. Spur tracks and sidings weave in and out among the various structures. While structures on the main street are in a row, others are aligned perpendicular to the main street, giving the town more depth.

▼ At Maple Estates, the homes in the background are on their foundations. There is an empty lot on the left where another building is placed for open houses. This building is normally stored indoors, but with a foundation in place, it is easily installed when necessary.

7

Bases

I have used a variety of materials and methods for making bases. Two ways I've found to be the best are using a pre-cast stepping stone, cut to fit if necessary, or Durarock (a type of cement board) and mortar.

Using stepping stones or pavers is fairly easy—the only limitation is size. Most of these are 12" x 12" x 2" or 12" x 24" x 2". I use a wet saw (normally used to cut tile) to cut the pavers to size. To set the stones, I dig out the area where the stepper is going to be placed, then I use sand or soil to level the stepper. Once the stone has been leveled, I place the building on this pad.

Durarock is a cement product that cuts like drywall. You can use a drywall knife for straight edges or a saber saw for complicated shapes. I cut out the building's base, including walkways or other appendages (see the sidebar on page 74). Then I dig out the area where the base is going to be installed, down about 2". Next, I mix up a batch of mortar or concrete and fill the dug-out area with the mortar mix. I then push the Durarock shape into the wet mortar mix. Using a level, I level the Durarock, clean up the edges with a trowel and let the mortar cure. Once cured, the base is permanent. The main advantage to this method is that you can create a complex shape without the need to make a form, and it's easy to level the base, since you do not have to trowel wet mortar.

I light my structures, so I pre-drill a hole in the base through which I later pull the power cable. I like to leave a little extra wire sticking up.

Terrain

If you have uneven terrain to work with in your railway, take advantage of it. It is rare to find a truly flat spot. It's not uncommon in the full-size world to see structures stepped into a gentle hillside. In the case of an extreme slope, structures may be built on stilts. In some parts of my hometown, for instance, the street side of a house may be one story and the backside may have three or four stories. Houses in river country were often built on pilings. These types of foundations will give your town and buildings extra dimension.

Even in an industrial area, a little greenery will bring the scene to life.

Mixing in a few trees and some ground cover can bring a town scene to life. Here, a New Zealand tea tree is in full bloom. The ground cover helps to blend the scene together.

A great little maple (*Acer palmatum* 'Tama Hime') is planted next to the California Furniture store. These two items complement each other. The maple is more visible because it is next to a structure, and the scene is softened and given life by the presence of the maple tree. Green carpet is used in the background.

1. With Durarock, you can cut out structure bases just the way you want them, including walkways. These foundations are all cut and ready to be installed.

2. Here the Durarock has been laid out. Wires for lighting have been pulled up through a hole cut in the Durarock.

3. The Durarock has been cemented in place. Mortar was placed on the ground, then the Durarock pressed into the wet mortar. When the Durarock sheets were leveled, the excess mortar that oozed out along the edges was removed with a trowel.

4. The foundation is finished. The next step is to add good topsoil and plants in the areas surrounding the structure.

SECTION 2:
Accent plants around structures

We are going to examine accent or city trees—trees you would find near buildings, in and around towns, and next to farmhouses. You can find just about any species of tree growing domestically somewhere. Shown here are plants that can be used to simulate ordinary trees that might be found in someone's backyard, along a street, or in a city park—trees like oaks, maples, and magnolias, as well as shrubs and bushes.

Unlike forest trees, accent trees would not necessarily grow in tall, slender patterns. They might grow in an upright broom style or have interesting branch structures. I like to use these plants around buildings to give them life. Most homes have trees of some kind around them, as well as other large plant material. Even in the heart of a big city, you will find the so-called urban forest.

Trees help to soften the scene, making it come to life. They also give you opportunities to add little touches, like a tire swing or a picnic table under the shade of the spreading branches of a miniature tree.

I look for the following characteristics when selecting plants for use in the city or near buildings:

• The plant must have small leaves.
• If the plant has flowers, they must be small, too.
• Plants should have the proper branch structure. I like those that can be trained to look like small trees by developing a single trunk or an interesting forked trunk, so I look at the basic branch structure of the plant to see if this type of shaping will be possible. If you are using the plant as a shrub, this is not important.
• Trees should be slow growers—14" in 10 years, for example. Slow growers are much easier to keep under control, but are not as forgiving if you make a trimming mistake.
• Plants should not grow too tall. A consideration when placing plants around model structures is accessibility.

Plumosa Compressa (Bonsai) is an evergreen plant that can be shaped in many ways. Here, it has been allowed to grow multiple trunks, giving it an interesting structure.

A *Plumosa Compressa* stands in the backyard of a house. At the right is a cotoneaster. These two plants have been in the ground for 10 years. They are slow growers and can be kept in shape by occasional trimming.

Thyme-leaf cotoneaster (*Cotoneaster microphylla* 'Thymifolia') also makes a nice miniature tree. Its branches are fairly tough and point in many directions, so they must be trimmed frequently in order to keep them in the shape you want. Their leaves are small. For part of the growing season they will put out small red berries, so this plant can be used as an apple tree. Here, a cotoneaster is used as a shade tree.

A mature cotoneaster is growing to the right of the house. This tree has an interesting history. It was the victim of a full-size pine tree that fell on it in the mid-1990s. The falling tree split the small tree and crushed a miniature house next to it. Using green garden tape, the author bound the two halves together and the tree healed, showing how tough this little plant is.

A Hokkaido dwarf Chinese elm (*Ulmus parvifolia* 'Hokkaido'), trimmed to look like a little tree, is located next to the building. A word of caution on the Hokkaido elm: Its branches are tender and can be easily broken off if bumped. Try to plant them so they are clear of any traffic. The Hokkaido puts out all sorts of growth, including small leaves right at the trunk. These can be removed by rubbing them off with your fingers, or you can use a small Bonsai tool designed for this job. They can be trimmed to reveal their gnarly branches and trunk. The more you prune them, the more gnarly they get.

It may be hard to trim them. Slow-growing plants that don't get too tall will be a plus in the long run.

In the full-size world, trees can tower over buildings by 100 feet or more. However, this sometimes looks out of place in our scaled-down world. For example, if we took a full-size tree that was 100 feet tall and re-created it in ½" scale, it would be 50 inches tall. When placed next to a model structure, it would likely look out of place even though it is in scale. Smaller-than-true-scale trees look better. Trees that are 6 to 18 inches tall will be in keeping with the scene. Smaller-than-scale-size trees will always look right, since all trees start out as little ones.

There are literally thousands of plants that will work well as accent or city trees. There are far too many varieties to cover here, so I am limiting my list to a few favorites. Keep in mind that I live in a mild climate (California's San Francisco Bay area). Check plant labels to see if the plants you have chosen will be suitable for your climate. Most of my plant material comes from Miniature Plant Kingdom in Sebastopol, California.

There are several plants in the Chamaecyparis family that are well suited for use as accent plants. The *Chamaecyparis pisifera* 'Plumosa Compressa' makes a great broom-style tree. The trunk can be trained to grow straight upright, with the upper branches forming a nice, neat ball. These plants look especially nice when set into front- or backyard scenes. Plumosa Compressa is slow growing and does not require a lot of pruning once the tree has been shaped. Its branches grow tightly together, and I usually do not try to open them up, but rather let them form a tight ball. A little trimming around the edges from time to time will keep this tree in shape. It is also good to reach inside the ball of the tree and remove any dead needles by rubbing them off with your fingers.

A similar tree is the Seiju dwarf Chinese elm. It is not as gnarly as the Hokkaido. Compared to the Hokkaido, it has a relatively smooth trunk and its leaves are slightly larger and are longer in shape.

Hokkaido and Seiju elms make great-looking miniature trees. They can be trimmed to reveal their gnarly branches and trunk. This Hokkaido elm is more than 15 years old.

Dwarf hinoki cypress (*Chamaecyparis obtusa* 'Nana') makes a neat green ball and does not require a lot of trimming. It grows slowly and makes an excellent miniature bush.

Here, you can see just how small a miniature rose can be. This is a pink miniature named Trinket. Eventually, the flower will pop out and be the size of a dime. These can be made into little trees by removing extra branches as they shoot up from the root ball.

Dwarf flowering pomegranate (*Punica granatum* 'Nana') has a yellow-green color and red flowers that become miniature pomegranates. They can be kept small by trimming. The leaves stay small. The fruit will be out of scale, but can be removed.

Miniature fuschia can also be trained to grow like little trees. They have small flowers and seem to be in bloom most of the year. This plant will put out several trunks at ground level. You can cut off all but one to develop a single-trunk tree, or you can select three trunks and braid them. In time the trunks will grow into each other, giving an interesting twisted effect.

This miniature rose has been trained to look like a small tree. This is done by continually removing branches that stray from the desired form.

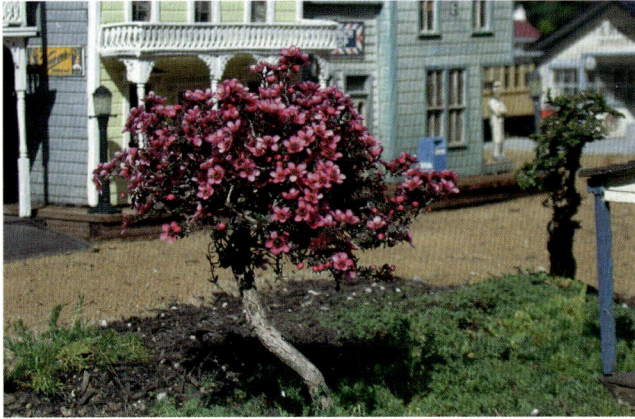

This dwarf New Zealand tea tree (*Leptospermum scoparium*) is a wonderful little plant that can be trimmed into a ball. It puts out beautiful little flowers once or twice a season. Its leaves are small, so the tree looks good even when not in full bloom.

Okinawa holly (*Ilex dimorphophylla*) makes an excellent little tree. Wear gloves when trimming—its leaves have little pincers. This tree can be opened up to show branch structure. It is relatively slow growing and doesn't require much trimming once you've established the basic shape. This one is more than 10 years old.

Examples of plants used in a scene

Pauline's Tea House is surrounded by several small plants that help bring life to the scene. The tree on the right is a Seiju elm, on the left is a Kingsville boxwood, while a dwarf Scot's heather is used as a bush on the left.

The scene of the three little pigs' houses uses several plants mentioned in this book. At the far left is a miniature fuchsia. The tree to the left of the house of straw is an Okinawa holly; on the right side is a snowrose. Between the house of sticks and the house of bricks is a *Chamaecyparis obtusa* 'Nana'. The plants in front of and alongside the brick house are *Chamaecyparis obtusa* 'Flabelliformis'. Dwarf mondo grass is used as a small, leafy ground cover. It is the spiky, grassy-looking plant.

◀ This scene depicts an industrial area on the author's railroad, the Crystal Spring Lumber Co., with the local auto repair shop and gasoline station in the foreground. The use of gold fines around the buildings suggests that this is an area where grass doesn't grow. The presence of the miniature trees brings life into a scene that otherwise might appear sterile.

Water feature design

The Kranen family's railway in California has tunnels and a water feature that were designed and built using the principles discussed in this chapter.

Water provides animation as well as sound in the garden railroad. I'll discuss ideas of how to integrate a water feature into a miniature landscape without overwhelming it. I'll also show you how to install and camouflage pond liners.

This is the future sight of the Kranen family's garden railroad and its water feature. The 1:1 track plan is in the process of being laid out with PVC pipe. This helps the designer in developing and visualizing the railway as it will ultimately appear.

Tunnels have been set in place with rocks and earth. This area is almost ready for construction to begin on the proposed water feature.

Water adds a great deal of interest to a garden railway. It is a form of animation that can act like a magnet, drawing you into the scene. It is also a source of sound and can have a soothing effect.

Most books on ponds are written to help a person design and install a fairly large garden pond or waterfall, usually intended to fill an area in a lawn. These are generally full-size replicas of streams, waterfalls, or ponds. Since these features are full size, a railway sometimes looks out of place with them, almost like the trains were an afterthought.

Another problem is that many of us don't have room to build this type of pond in our garden-railway area. Generally speaking, garden-railroad water features are smaller than other garden ponds. Articles on building these large water features are useful, though, as they provide a lot of good information that can be carried over into a garden-railroad water feature. Here, I will discuss building water features specifically for garden railroads.

It is always best to design and install a water feature early in the building process. Laying out your track plan using PVC pipe, as described in Chapter 1, will help in planning your water feature's design.

I think flowing water in a garden railroad is as interesting as, or even more interesting, than a pond. In fact, you could consider the pond simply as a water-collection basin necessary to operate a waterfall or stream—albeit a basin that should be decorated and blended into the surrounding scene.

In practice, you can design a water system without a pond by creating a cistern to collect the water. This is not to say you can't build an impressive pond, but I think one should put as much or more effort into designing the waterfall or stream to provide motion. I have two ponds on my Crystal Springs Railroad; one is a small mountain lake and the other is a log pond.

To create a natural-looking water flow, you must incorporate some elevation into your railroad design. When designing a water feature with a waterfall, you should create the largest mountain the area will support. This will give you a place to start a watercourse and room to develop a pleasing water flow.

Waterfalls

High in the mountains, even the largest real-life waterfalls and rivers begin in small crevices. When rain falls or snow melts, these crevices become streams that feed a system of larger crevices, which in turn become larger streams that feed into creeks and rivers that eventually flow to the sea. Obviously, we can't model an entire water system, but understanding how this system works will help you design your water feature.

The first thing to understand is that waterfalls do not start at the tops of mountains like volcanoes. Yes, there are some waterfalls that may appear that way—Bridal Veil Falls in Yosemite, for example. There, the water drops over a sharp cliff, but what you don't see is several miles of higher ground from which the water has drained. The same is true with Niagara Falls. If viewed from below from the *Maid of the Mist*, the water would seem to be flowing from the top of a mountain, but when seen as it really is, water from miles away drains into a river that eventually drops over the falls. Most of us do not have enough room to create this type of waterfall.

Even though this is a small water feature, by curving the waterway, several viewing angles can be achieved. Notice that the water's source is hidden from view. The water appears to be coming from around the bend, which gives the illusion that there is more beyond the line of sight.

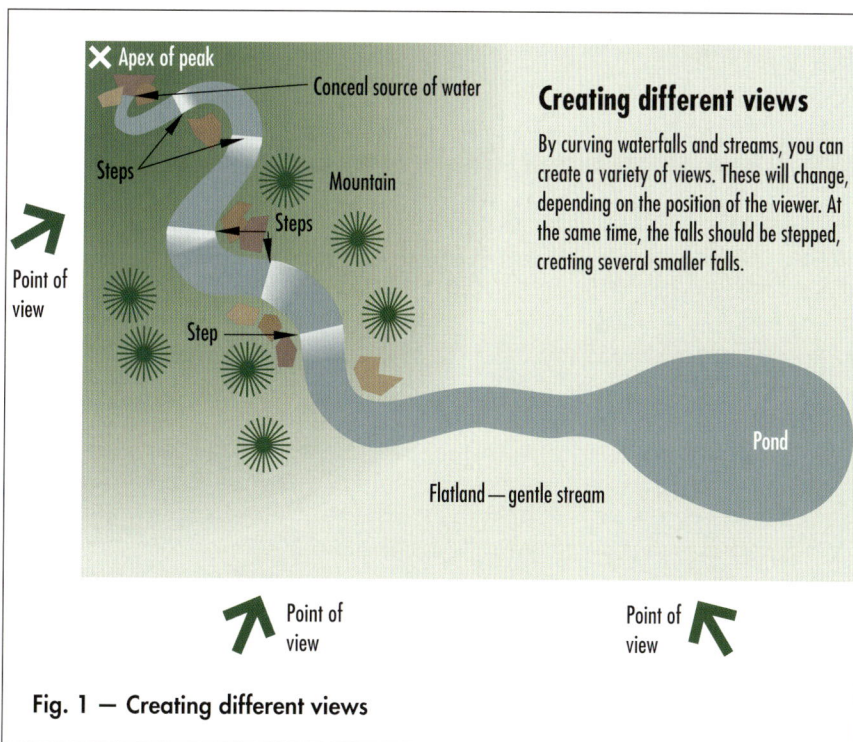

Creating different views

By curving waterfalls and streams, you can create a variety of views. These will change, depending on the position of the viewer. At the same time, the falls should be stepped, creating several smaller falls.

Fig. 1 — Creating different views

SECTION 2:
Design principles and waterfalls

Instead of a normal garden water feature, we are striving to create one that will enhance our miniature landscape. This means building the water feature in scale. When I say "scale" in this context, I do not mean it literally. I mean that the water feature should be designed to complement the trains so that everything looks reasonably proportioned. Don't use river rocks the

size of scale SUVs as river sand. Rather, use aquarium sand, which looks like (and actually is) miniature river rock.

Keep plants along the streambed small. Real railroads cross far more small streams and creeks than large bodies of water. (This is true of highways, too.) It's easier to work a small waterway into the scene than a large one. Of course, if you have the space and want to model Niagara Falls, go for it.

Once you've determined where the track levels are going to be, you can establish the location of the waterfalls, the streambed, and the pond or cistern. At first, the water feature will be nothing more than a ditch. However, this ditch must be made correctly. It must be much larger and deeper than the finished feature will be. This is because you will be placing "gulapata" (my special concrete mix—see sidebar below) and rock over the liner, so your finished waterway will end up smaller.

Another concern is grading. Water naturally only flows downhill; you must lay out the future stream so the water will flow properly. Generally, the grade should be no less than a ¼"-per-foot drop. Also, try to angle the side walls of the ditch and pond so that the rubber liner will bed in more easily. If the walls are too steep, this could result in an air pocket between the liner and the ground.

Gulapata will serve as a decorative lining, and it also will protect the actual liner. You can use gulapata to form waterfalls, streambeds, and the banks of streams. You can either sculpt pure gulapata to shape or you can use both rocks and gulapata together. I prefer the latter method.

In some cases, an underlayment should be used. This is necessary when installing a water feature in native soil that's been freshly excavated, to protect the liner from sharp rocks. You can purchase an underlayment that is made of a felt-like material, or you can create your own by using an old rug, carpet padding, newspapers, or wet sand. The idea is to provide a smooth surface on which the liner can rest. When building a water feature in fresh fill, an underlayment may not be necessary.

Waterfall design

When designing a garden-railroad waterfall, as opposed to a small full-size water feature for your lawn, a more practical approach is to design a small mountain waterfall, one that might be part of system of many that feeds a stream, creek, or river. Here are some techniques for creating the illusion that your waterfall is natural (**fig. 1**).

• Start your waterfall somewhere below the top of the mountain.

• Design the water discharge (source of the watercourse) so it cannot be seen from normal viewing angles.

• Curve the waterways. Since you cannot see around corners, curves help create the illusion that the water is flowing from a distant place.

• Create several smaller falls, or drops, rather than one huge drop. When designed correctly, you will see different waterfalls as you change viewing positions.

• Make the falls using rock similar to that found in surrounding areas.

• Color the cement to match the surrounding area.

• Add small rocks to the bottom of the streambed.

• Plant trees and ground cover as close as possible to the water's edge.

• Avoid the levee look—where space permits, the surrounding landscape should be higher than the streambed. Levees are okay when the stream or creek runs though a town, where the residents may have installed one.

• To keep things in proportion or scale, use small water plants and small fish. Duckweed makes a good scale-model water lily. Keep it under control by simply scooping out the excess. Guppies or mosquito fish make excellent scale trout. I find guppies interesting, since they often swim in schools and even try to swim upstream. Guppies also eat mosquito larvae.

• When creating the bottom of your pond, make a low spot in which to set your pump and filter. This will also serve as a point where a sump pump can be placed to drain the pond.

A waterfall can simply fall into a concealed basin and end there, or you can create a decorative pond. Space permitting, you can create a stream to route the water to a pond located several feet away from the waterfall.

▶ This is a double waterfall. One pump and filter provide water for both falls. There is a "T" to divide the water between streams. A PVC valve can be installed to regulate the flow between the two falls.

Using gulapata

To make mountains and other artificial rock features, I mix a material I call "gulapata." The formula is one 60-pound sack of mortar, one shovelful of fire clay, and ⅓-shovel of Portland cement (a little more or less will still work). Mix the ingredients as you would concrete. The result is a creamy, sticky mixture to spread over a base coat of stucco or directly onto a project.

Using a scoop or trowel and a large paintbrush, spread the gulapata on like very thick cake frosting. The trick is in the final application, which you can sculpt to look like rock. You can use almost any tool to sculpt and shape this mixture before it cures. A paintbrush, a wooden spatula, a stiff bristle brush, a putty knife, or a sponge can create interesting textures. Another way to create texture is to use overlay molds made of aluminum foil. Crumple the foil, then lay it over the wet mixture. After 5 to 15 minutes, depending on the weather, the mixture will begin to harden. This is the best time to do the texturing. If you do it too soon, the mixture will stick to the laid-over mold or the tools; if you wait too long, the

mixture will be too hard to work. Experiment on a small area first. If you don't like the results, cement over it and start again.

Color is the key to aesthetic success. Without color, the gulapata will look like cement. The simple method is to add concrete dye to the ingredients as you mix them. This will create a base color. You can add other colors about one hour after the gulapata has been applied by spraying it with concrete dye mixed with water. Use a common spray bottle or garden sprayer. You can also paint gulapata after it dries.

Gulapata also can be used in the construction of ponds and waterfalls to make artificial rock formations. A close cousin to gulapata is "Sona stone." This is a mixture of 3 parts water, 2 parts vermiculite, and 1 part Portland cement. This mixture can be applied to a surface or hand-molded into shape. Allow it to cure overnight, then carve it using a sharp object such as an ice pick, awl, or dental pick. This material is useful in making simulated cut stonework such as railroad bridges and retaining walls.

Soil and rocks have been built up in the area where the waterway will be. The freshly dug ditch is wider and deeper than the finished waterway will be.

Dart and Dot Rinefort's waterfall is a relatively small one. It brings to mind waterfalls seen along the Durango & Silverton route through the Animas River Canyon during the spring thaw. Several small waterfalls are better than one big one.

This water feature has a natural look to it. It illustrates that, with attention to detail and track placement, a large area isn't necessary to make an effective water feature.

SECTION 3:
Constructing watercourses

When I first started building water features, I made them out of concrete and used watertight sealing paint to waterproof them. Concrete ponds can be made waterproof this way, but making streams and waterfalls watertight is another thing. It is nearly impossible, on a small scale, to make an all-concrete waterfall or stream watertight.

I hesitated to use rubber pond liners because they are difficult to hide. The instructions that come with them caution you against cutting the liner. It seemed impossible to use a rubber pond liner to create anything other than the same old semi-round, ordinary garden-variety pond.

Then I discovered peel-and-stick roofing tape, available from roofing-supply houses. This is a rubber-like tape about 12" wide. It has a very sticky adhesive and is used to splice rubber roofing materials. With the ability to cut and splice a liner, I was now free to create streams and waterfalls by cutting the liner to the size I wanted, then splicing it to the pond's liner. Since I first started doing this, a double-sided peel-and-stick tape has been introduced specifically for pond liners. I have tried it, and it works well—even better than the roofing tape.

When splicing, try to make the splice in an area that is not normally under water when the stream or waterfall is not running. For example, do not splice the liner inside the pond itself. Instead, lead the pond's liner up and into the waterway and splice it in the streambed. The idea is to have the splice high and dry when the pump that runs the waterfall and stream is turned off.

It is best to splice liner pieces in place. Lay the liner in position where it is to be installed. Work it in as close to its final placement as possible. At the point where you are going to make the splice, place a board under the liner to serve as a working surface. Lay the two pieces of liner to be spliced on the board, with the upstream piece over the downstream piece, as you would a shingle. Clean the surface to be spliced with a good cleaning solvent, like MEK or lacquer thinner. This will ensure a tight bond.

Cut the tape to length, then peel off enough of the backing at one end to just start the tape seam. Rub the tape down on the joint at one end, then reach under the tape and pull the backing film off as you smooth down the tape joint. Now rub the tape down more firmly to form a tight seal. This is best done on a warm day. If it's cool outside, you can use a hair dryer to warm the seam. When hot, the tape's adhesive is very tacky. In fact, on really hot days, it can be difficult to pull the protective covering off, so you may have to put the tape in the refrigerator for a while to make it easier to remove the protective covering. Apply the tape as above, but wait for it to warm up again before finally pressing it down.

The most difficult part of using a pond liner for a streambed is hiding it. The liner's instructions tell you to fold and manipulate the liner and to place rocks along the edge to conceal it. This technique works fine for a regular semi-round pond, but it is nearly impossible to hide the liner if you want to be creative and have twisting, turning waterways, especially on a smaller-size water feature.

I used to make my water features out of cement. When making a stream or waterfall with cement, it is easy to free-form it into the shape you want. The biggest problem with cement, though, is making it watertight. Water will not seep through the cement itself, but cracks often form in the cement that allow leakage.

I now combine the two processes. I lay down the liner as closely as possible to the shape I want, using the splicing method described above. Then I use my gulapata cement mixture and rocks to create my water-feature details. In the process, the cement covers the liner completely. If the gulapata happens to crack, it doesn't matter, since we are not depending on it for waterproofing.

When using a cement product, it can sometimes be a problem if you

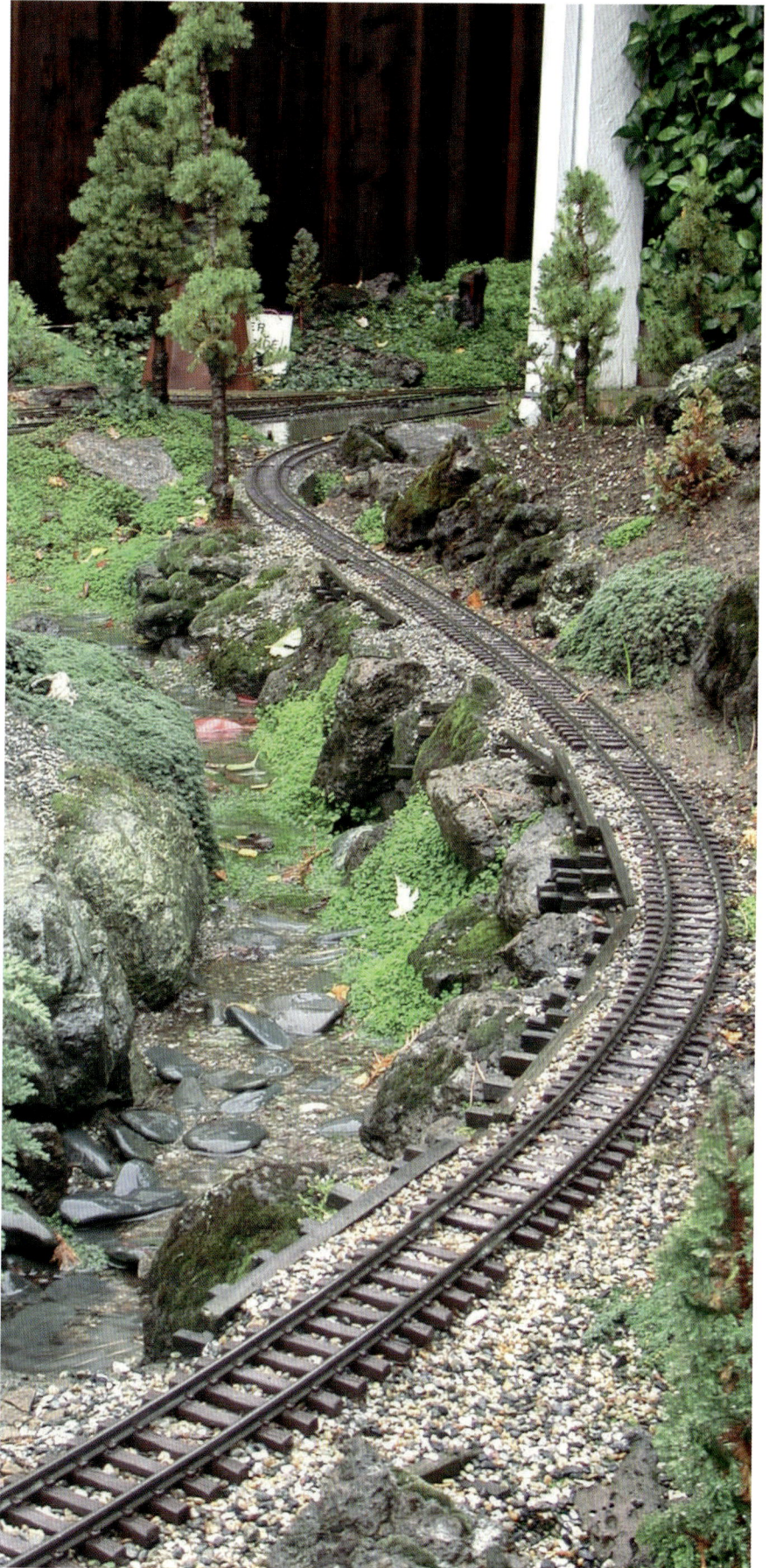

The dry wash on the left side of the track adds interest to the scene and also provides an actual drainage path for lawn sprinkling and downpours.

On Don and Fatima Marquardt's garden railway, the watercourse behind the trestle was built by the author using the methods described here.

The liner has been cut to fit the waterway. In this case, two pieces of liner have been spliced together using seaming tape.

Pond liner seaming tape is used to join pieces of liner together. This is a double-sided tape.

want to test the water flow and alter it by cementing rocks in place. It takes about 24 hours for regular cement to cure enough to run water over it. Sometimes it is helpful to use hydraulic cement (cement that will harden under water) to fine-tune your water system. You can cement rocks in place to re-route water using this hydraulic cement. It cures quickly and can even be used in areas that are wet or under water, which can be helpful when you want to test the water flow immediately. It is impractical, though, to use hydraulic cement for anything other than small areas, such as patching or for holding rocks in place. It is usually sold in small amounts, typically five-pound buckets.

You may want to put aquarium sand in your streambed to represent the thousands of pieces of river rock that generally line the bottoms of waterways. You can simply throw the sand in. If the stream is not too swift, the sand will stay in place. If you want to glue the sand down, adhere it with concrete adhesive. It is best to keep the newly glued area dry for several days before allowing water to flow over the work. I recommend doing this during hot weather, as the heat will accelerate the curing time. The adhesive will not cure in cold weather.

Sound

Sound is created when water falls or is agitated. It can be amplified by giving your water feature steeper sides, in effect making a small amphitheater. You can use gulapata to form these areas. A series of small waterfalls and small pools will look good and add sound.

Another sound-producing device is an agitator. This is a small, raised lip at the waterfall's edge that agitates the water and causes it to ripple and eddy. This also adds visual interest.

Dry washes

A dry wash can be considered a "water" feature. Even though it is dry, it is shaped in much the same way as a stream or river. A dry wash can often look more realistic than a feature with water in it. Because you don't have to worry about a liner and waterproofing, you are free to arrange rocks just as you want them.

The author covers the liner completely with rock and mortar (gulapata). The main problem with liners, especially in small ponds, is hiding them. Rocks and mortar do the job.

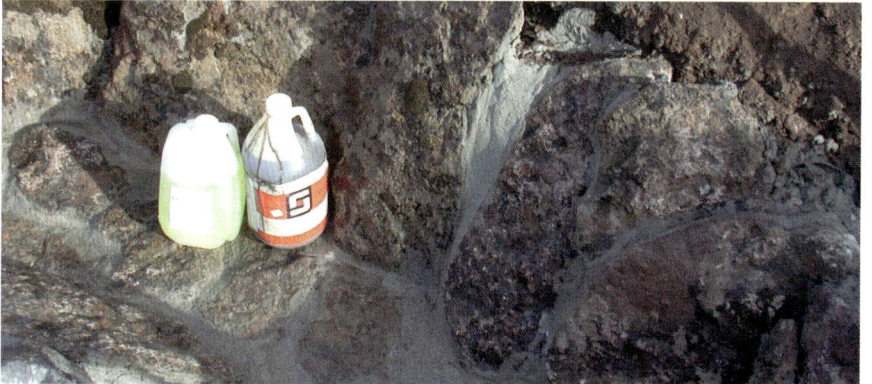

After the mortar sets, the excess is cleaned from the rocks with a scraper and a wire brush. A solution of one part muriatic acid and four parts water is used to remove the cement residue. Use caution when using muriatic acid and be sure to wear protective gear, including gloves, safety glasses, and a respirator. The acid is washed off with fresh water. The author colors the mortar using Lithchrome Chemstain, an acid-based stain that will color cured cement.

Two stages of the process. At left, the rock and mortar have been placed but not cleaned or colored. On the right side, the rocks have been cleaned and the first application of color has been applied. The PVC pipe has been re-attached to the grade stake to get a fix on where the roadbed will be. The red flags mark the location of the grade stakes.

SECTION 4:
Liners, pumps, and filters

In this section, I'll be discussing the use of pond liners, pumps, and filters. I refer to brand names and model numbers for identification and specification purposes. I have had good results with these products, but there are other brands that should work equally well.

The liner material I prefer is a 45-mil (.045"-thick) rubber, Tetra 45 MIL EPDM Liner. Liners made from EPDM (ethylene-propylene-diene monomer) offer greater flexibility than PVC (polyvinyl chloride) liners. This is important, because half the battle in building a good-looking waterway is hiding the liner. Even if you will be covering the liner with mortar, you still must be able to fold and shape it. If you use a stiffer liner, this compounds the problem. On the other hand, for durability I would not use anything less than the 45-mil thickness.

If you are laying a liner over fresh fill or sandy soil, you do not need an underlayment, especially if you are covering the liner with mortar. If you are working in rocky soil, a layer of wet sand, old carpet, or newspaper will act as an underlayment. The idea is to provide a barrier between any sharp objects and the liner.

Tetra makes a 3"-wide, double-sided seaming tape that will join most pond liners. It works on both EPDM and PVC liners. As mentioned earlier, peel-and-stick roofing tape will also work.

Pumps
Pumps are available in a variety of styles and capacities for your waterworks. I prefer to use submersible pumps, which can be placed at the bottom of a pond. This helps eliminate complicated plumbing as well as the need to pierce the pond liner to make a drain hole.

The most important thing to consider in selecting the correct pump is its capacity, expressed as gallons per hour (GPH). This figure is variable, depending on your waterworks' design. The GPH posted on the pump is based on what the pump puts out at the discharge. It does not take "head" into consideration.

▲ On the Rinefort's railroad (San Rafael, California), water runs through a long stream that runs parallel to the railroad in certain areas. Notice the use of Cold Water Canyon rocks. These are flat rocks that have been assembled using gulapata colored with Lithchrome Chemstain.

Head is the vertical distance the water must be pumped. For example, if your waterfall is five feet higher than your pump, you have a five-foot head to overcome. Each pump includes a chart showing its GPH rating at various heights. For instance, a pump rated at 500 GPH with no head is rated for only 25 GPH at a 15-foot head.

The amount of water flow coming out of your waterfall or stream is based on two factors: the size of your water feature (mainly the width of it) and the head. Some people want a rushing torrent of water, as would be seen during a spring thaw. Others prefer a smaller flow, simulating what you might see later in the year. The water flow can be controlled by selecting the right size pump. It is better to choose a larger pump than a smaller one, since you can always throttle back a larger pump if necessary.

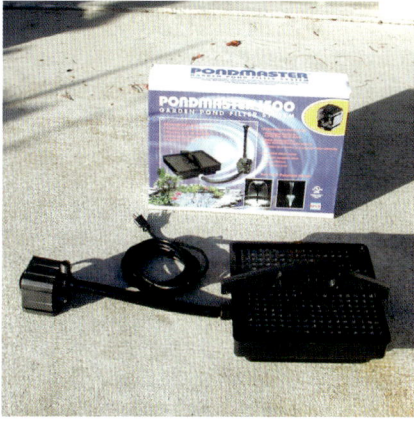

This is the Pond Master 1500 system, which includes a 500 GPH pump. It is an ideal small-pond system (but not for fish ponds). It provides both mechanical and biological filtration and will need to be cleaned every three to five weeks or so, depending on the season.

A Pond Master 1000 filter has been adapted to work with a larger Cal 1200 GPH pump and set in place. The power cord and water-discharge hose go through a two-inch PVC elbow embedded in mortar. The author uses clear plastic hose up to the hard pipe. The hard pipe runs up to the top of the water feature to save money.

The pump I use most frequently is a Cal Pump S1200T-20. This stainless-steel-and-bronze pump is rated at 1200 GPH for one foot of lift. I use this pump even for smaller applications because I can lower the output using a butterfly valve mounted at the discharge. If the pump you select does not have a built-in valve, you can install a clamp-down restrictor on the discharge hose to control the flow, or you can install a valve in the discharge line. Never restrict the intake side of the pump.

Filters and strainers

The ponds I am discussing here are not designed for koi (or any type of fish). If you intend to keep koi, you will have to design your pond to accommodate them. Koi ponds must be deep and their sides should be sheer to prevent raccoons and other animals from fishing from the banks. The most important thing for a koi pond is the filtration system, which is often as large as the pond itself and is beyond the scope of this book. There are other books available that can assist you.

For non-koi ponds, filtration is still necessary, but on a smaller scale. The filter's main function is to keep debris out of the pump. Minimum filtration would be a suction strainer. This type of filtration is called mechanical. Most pumps will come with a basic strainer.

Cal Pump offers a heavy-duty filter strainer for its pumps. In smaller ponds,

a Supreme Pondmaster 1000 pad filter works well. It is a simple 12" x 12" box with a polyester and activated-charcoal filter. It is rated at 700 GPH, but I have run adapted 1200 GPH pumps to them with good results. This is a complete filtration system, which means it is also a biological filter that uses bacteria to break down pond waste. Clean the filter by removing the polyester filter material and washing it with a high-pressure garden hose.

Hose and tubing

Plumbing a submersible pump is relatively easy. If you are using a pad-type filter, you'll need a hose to connect the pump to the filter. One is usually supplied with the filter. You'll then need a hose to feed the waterfall. I try to find a hose that will fit directly over the discharge port, which is usually a ½" pipe thread. This normally takes a hose with a ¾" inside diameter.

I connect one end of the hose, using a clamp, to the pump. If you are doing a short run, you can use hose all the way to the head of the waterfall. On longer runs I use PVC pipe, which is less expensive (about 10 cents per foot compared to about $1 per foot for hose). I connect a hose from the pump to the PVC pipe, then run the pipe to the head area of the waterfall. I then connect another hose to the discharge end of the PVC pipe. This gives me flexibility where I need it and allows me

to remove the discharge hose to pump out the pond or back-flush the system.

At the headwaters, where the hose enters the water feature, I create a hole in which the hose can be inserted and kept in place. It is best to do this when making the waterway. You can cement in a pipe that is large enough for the tubing to fit through. I also do this at the pond end. I use a plastic electrical-conduit elbow that's large enough for the pump's power cord and plug, as well as the hose, to fit through. The elbow is cemented in place and covered with rocks so it is not visible.

Draining the pond

The above system does not incorporate a drain, so you'll have to work out a system to drain your pond. This must be done from time to time, depending on your area and conditions. One way is to use your pond pump. You can do this by adding an extension hose to the waterfall end of the system and routing the water into a bucket or drain. This usually gets the water level to within a couple inches of the bottom. You can bail the remaining water by hand.

Another method of draining the pond is with a siphon. When using a siphon, I fit a filter of some kind on the end of the hose that goes into the pond to keep debris from clogging the hose.

The best way to drain a pond is with a sump pump. You can get right down to the bottom with this device.

8

SECTION 5:
Loose ends

In this section, I'll try to tie up some loose ends about pond construction.

Using foam caulking

Once your waterway is finished, you may want to place rocks in it to help route the water and create interest. A problem when doing this is holding the rocks in place. Flowing water tends to move rocks downstream. Using mortar to hold small rocks has the disadvantage that it takes 24 hours to set up enough to test the flow. This makes minor adjustments time consuming.

I found an interesting product called "EnerFoam," manufactured by Dow Products (**photo 1**). EnerFoam is used to (among other things) seal leaks around windows and doors, seal out insects and rodents around drain and water pipes, and secure drywall. It is a fast-curing foam that can be trimmed in less than one hour. EnerFoam is applied much like caulk, except that it is under pressure, so you only have to pull the trigger to apply it. It cures and becomes waterproof quickly. You can place a rock in your stream, secure it, and test the water flow, all within an hour.

The streambed in cross section

The drawing (**fig. 2**) shows a typical section of a streambed. Note that the ditch in which the stream lies is much larger than the finished streambed. Mortar has been used to line the liner and to hold the rocks in place. The drawing is exaggerated to more clearly show the size differences. It is important that the liner's edges are higher than the waterline so that water will not wick under it.

Aquascape

Photo 2 shows the Aquascape skimmer. This unit is installed at the pond end of the system so it skims water from the surface of the pond. The trap door on the left is connected to the pond by means of a special watertight flange system. This allows you to cut a hole in the liner to allow water to enter the skimmer through the trap door. The water is pre-filtered through the fiber filter pad. Next to the skimmer box is a net that is installed inside the skimmer to catch leaves and other debris.

With the pre-filter pad removed (**photo 3**), you can see the skimmer system's pump. The discharge hose will eventually enter through the large hole at the upper right. It will be connected to the elbow that is attached to the pump. The other large hole can be used for the optional automatic filler and can serve as an overflow.

Photo 4 shows the Aquascape filter, an excellent filter system. Water enters the bottom of the box and percolates up through several fiber filter pads and through a layer of lava rock. The filtered water then overflows the lip. This filter is installed at the high end of the system at the source of your waterfall or stream. The only problem I found with this system is its large size. To hide the filter, you must build up the area around it. If you have the space, this is not a problem, and the filter could even serve as a lake.

The EnerFoam system can be used to secure rocks to streambeds.

This is the Aquascape skimmer. The white pad inside is a pre-filter.

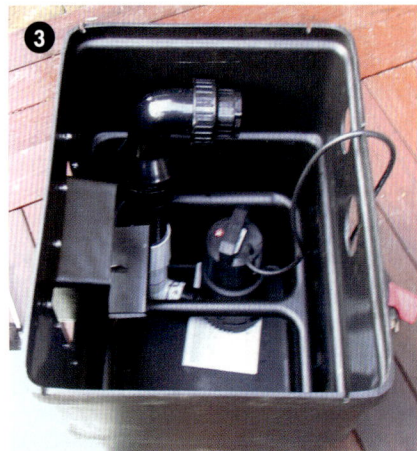

The pump (center) resides in the bottom of the skimmer tank.

The Aquascape filter system is excellent. Its only drawback is its size.

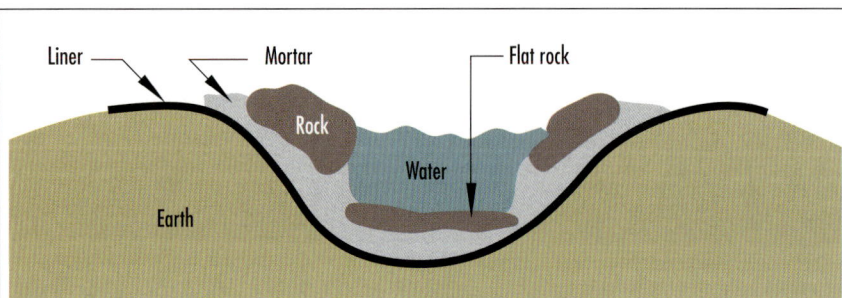

Liner — Mortar — Flat rock

Rock

Water

Earth

Fig. 2 — Streambed cross section

CHAPTER 9

Maintaining your railway

An electric fence can be an effective deterrent to animal incursion. The one described here can easily be removed, replaced, and repositioned.

A little routine maintenance goes a long way in the garden. This chapter shows some quick and easy ways to take care of your pond and garden, as well as some tips on how to control the critters that might find their way into your yard.

SECTION 1:
Gardening tools

Tools like the ones shown above are used to keep our trees in proper shape, for planting new plants, for weeding, and for trimming.

1 A good pair of shears is a must. I prefer ones with pointed tips, which allow you to get into tight areas. They can be used to trim off small branches to about ⅜" thick, although larger branches can be cut with a little more effort. They are also useful for trimming growth at the ends of the branches. Their relatively small size makes them easy to handle. I prefer those with flexible plastic handles, which are much more comfortable than the steel-handle versions.

2 Branch cutters or nippers are used to cut branches off a tree's trunk. They provide more leverage than shears do when cutting large-diameter branches. A branch cutter is a must when trimming trees like Alberta spruce, which have tough branches.

3 Nippers are a cleanup tool used to remove nubs left behind by other cutters. They cut down into the tree's trunk. When the tree

heals, the bark will cover the scar. If done correctly, the places where branches have been removed will barely be visible.

4 A limb saw is a small folding saw that fits in your pocket. It works well on smaller trees, and its size allows you to get into tight areas. A limb saw is handy when you need something a little bigger to remove a branch or extra trunks.

5 I use grass shears to trim ground cover, especially thyme, baby tears, and chamomile. Notice that the handle and blade are offset. This makes them more comfortable to use, which is important if you have a lot of trimming to do.

6 Battery-powered grass trimmers make the job of trimming ground cover fast and easy. This model comes with a long-handle attachment (not shown) that allows you to use it while standing.

7 The best feature of this battery-powered hedge trimmer is its compact size. It is great for trimming miniature hedges and certain trees. Its small size makes it easy to wield. I would not recommend it for large hedging jobs, but it is great for small ones. If you have topiaries, this is a good detailing tool.

8 A bulb planter is used to make a hole

suitable for planting bulbs or small plants. Push and turn it into the ground, then pull it out. It will remove a plug of soil, leaving a hole the size of a 3" pot.

Also, with this tool you can remove a plug of ground cover for transplanting. Release the plug by pushing it up from the bottom and removing it from the top. Next, use the tool to make a new hole. Place the plug in the new hole, using the soil that was removed to fill the old one. Doing this is beneficial for the old ground cover because it allows it to add new growth and provides places for it to spread out.

9 A dibble is used to create a small planting hole and is useful in and among rocks where it's difficult to dig. It makes a hole by wallowing out the soil.

10 The Garden Scoop, by Garden Works in Bellevue, Washington, is the greatest little garden shovel I have ever used. A combination spade and scoop, it's curved like a scoop, but with a point like a spade, making it an efficient digging tool that also allows you to remove materials with ease. It is difficult to remove the soil from a hole with a straight trowel, while a regular scoop has no point and isn't designed for digging. This tool combines the best of both. As an extra bonus, it has a serrated edge that is useful for cutting through small roots.

11 A root-combing tool is used to break up root-bound root balls.

12 This homemade weeder is similar to a large root-combing tool. I use it for both weeding and digging. It used to be a three-tine tool. I push the single tine into the ground and move it around under the weed, which loosens it right up. This tool also works on weeds in the roadbed. I go in under the track from the side. Because the tine is small, it can be extracted with a minimal amount of disturbance.

13 This is a combination weeder and sickle, useful for clearing away grasslike weeds. The sickle part has a serrated edge that helps cut through tough weeds and roots. The forked end is used to pull up weeds. The curved design means that you must buy either a right- or left-hand version. I have one of each. I find that when working around garden railroads, you usually do not have clear access to everything. Sometimes you have to use this tool in the opposite hand to reach into an area.

14 A combination tool can be handy. It folds up small enough to put in your pocket or on your belt. However, like most combination tools, there are certain compromises that have to be made. For example, I would not want to use the branch cutter all day long,

since a dedicated branch cutter would be more comfortable to use. Its main advantage is that you can keep it with you and, when you see something that needs immediate attention, you can take care of it. It can save you several trips back and forth for different tools since it has a weeder, a small branch nipper, a straight knife blade, and a serrated knife blade with a pointed tip.

15 This collapsible cuttings container is made of lightweight fabric. You throw cuttings in it while on site. It is larger and lighter than a five-gallon plastic bucket and is easy to move around with you as you trim your trees. If storage space is limited, it can be collapsed and stored flat.

16 A garden sprayer is handy for applying fertilizer, insecticide, and weed killer. You should have a separate sprayer for each use. In practice, I only use this type of sprayer for Roundup, a herbicide. The sprayer shown here has been customized for using Roundup around ornamental plants. Roundup kills everything that has foliage. By installing a funnel around the spray head, I can control the back splash and drift that would normally occur when using a sprayer. This allows me to get in between good plants and to spray weeds without harming surrounding plants. In some cases, I surround the weed by placing the funnel on the

ground and then spraying. This ensures that the weed gets a good dose while protecting the surrounding area. A word of caution: Roundup is a systemic herbicide. It will kill the plant down to the roots. If you spray it on ground covers, it will kill not only in the spot you hit directly, but a larger area surrounding the hit area, too. This effect can be minimized if you take a spade and cut the surrounding roots by driving it into the ground around the area you intend to hit.

SECTION 2:
Pond maintenance

There will always be a certain amount of sediment and muck in a water feature. This is natural and should be of no concern. Personally, I don't like my pond to be too clean. I prefer a little green, which helps hide the pond's bottom. However, it's still necessary to clean the pond from time to time to keep pumps and filters flowing. Once a year is usually sufficient.

Pond-maintenance tools
Here are some of the items I use for pond maintenance. The first is a small

1 This small surface skimmer is used to remove floating debris.

2 A wire-mesh wastebasket is used as a coarse filter to protect the pump or siphon hose from clogging with debris.

3 Ordinary pond-cleaning items. On the left, the cat-litter scoop and plastic dust pan are useful for cleaning debris and muck from the pond bottom. The dust pan will catch water as well as debris. The colander is used to drain water from the muck so you can re-use the muck in your topsoil.

hand-held skimming net (**photo 1**). I use one intended for swimming pools. This is useful for skimming surface debris, such as pine needles, leaves, and other garbage that seems to find its way into the water.

One way to drain a pond is to use a hose to siphon out the water. The only drawback is that you must have some grade, since you must siphon the water to a point lower than the pond. Another method is to use a sump pump. This will quickly drain a pond and will allow you to run the water off wherever you want it. You can use this waste water to irrigate your garden, or you can run it into a drain.

One potential problem with both methods is debris getting into the line or pump and clogging the system. I found a simple, inexpensive solution—a metal mesh wastebasket (**photo 2**). I place the basket in the pond, then place the pump in the basket. This keeps large debris from getting sucked into the pump. You can do the same thing with the end of the siphon hose.

To set up a siphon, I hook a garden hose up to the hose bib. I place the other end into the wastebasket, making sure the hose end is all the way down to the bottom of the basket (I use a rock to hold down the hose end). Then I turn on the water. Once all the air has been expelled from the line and water is going into the pond, I turn the water off and unscrew the hose from the hose bib. As long as the hose-bib end of the hose is below the pond's level, the water will start running out of the pond. If the end of the hose outside the pond is not below grade, disconnect the hose, then quickly put your thumb over the hose end until you can move that end to an area that is below pond level. Be sure to flush out the hose with fresh water when you are finished.

If you have fish, they'll need to be removed before draining the water. I have guppies in my pond, so I drain my pond about two-thirds of the way, then fish the guppies out with a net. The less water there is, the easier it is to catch the fish. Keep your fish in a bucket or other container full of water taken from the pond—don't use fresh water.

Once the water is down as far as it can be drained with the hose or pump,

I use a plastic cat-litter scoop (**photo 3**) to pick up any large debris that has accumulated at the bottom of the pond. Once this is out, I switch to a rubber dust pan, using it as a scoop to remove the sludge. I suggest looking through the debris. You will often find missing parts and, sometimes, miniature people that have fallen in.

I use a colander to drain the water from the debris, then I pile up the debris to dry. I use it later as part of my topsoil, since most of the debris is topsoil to begin with.

Our local water company adds chloramine (chlorine and ammonia) to purify the water. I am told this will kill the fish, so a dechlorinator must be used. I use AquaSafe Pond Water Conditioner. Check with your water company to see if they are using chloramine or chlorine. I let my pond water circulate for a day or two before returning the fish.

Unsightly, annoying foam will sometimes develop on the surface of a pond. I found an additive called Fountain Care Anti-Foam that works well. By adding one teaspoon per gallon of water, foam is eliminated immediately.

SECTION 3:
Protecting your pond and garden from pests

Water tends to attract animals. Some animals can be destructive. I have found a couple of ways to deal with them.

Recently, we were invaded by raccoons. They came into our yard, dug up ground cover, pulled up small trees, and generally made a mess. I saw a device called a Scarecrow. This is a self-contained sprinkler equipped with a motion sensor. When motion is detected, the device shoots a high-powered stream of water for three seconds. It then resets and does it again if something is still present after nine seconds.

When an animal was in the protected zone (about 180 degrees in front of the device), it would get a blast of water and would go away. The only problem was that the raccoons figured out where the protected zones were, so they would come in behind the Scarecrow and destroy the areas in the blind spots. The problem was getting enough Scarecrows to protect my area. I was up to four of them before I decided to take more drastic action. I believe that for most applications, the Scarecrow would be sufficient protection.

Instead, I ran an electric wire through the garden, near the areas the invaders like to visit. While this did not form a complete perimeter, it became, in effect, a trip wire. My thinking was to just put it where they are likely to run into it. So far, this has worked. I first installed the wire using a combination of ordinary hardware items that I had on hand, along with an electric-fence controller. This method can be used to install a fence around a pond to keep pets and wild animals from entering the pond area.

I bought an electric-fence controller and a roll of electric-fence wire. I found two types of controllers at a local hardware store. One was an intimidating system used for cattle and sheep, while the second unit was designed for pets and small animals. I decided on the smaller pet unit. The unit I bought was a "K-9 Electric Fence Controller" manufactured by Zareba. It was a surprisingly lightweight and compact unit. This system does not require any dedicated grounding rod: it uses the electric-utilities grounding system. There is one lug, to which you connect the fence wire. Then it is plugged into a standard 110V outlet.

Most important is the fence installation itself. Although simple, it must be done correctly. The principle is to run a bare wire from point to point, to form a barrier with which the animal will come in contact. The wire must be totally insulated from ground, which means no contact with plants, weeds, or any other grounded objects. The wire becomes part of a large capacitor that will discharge its energy through the offending animal when it comes in contact with it. The 1,000 volts will shock but not kill an animal, since the amperage is very low.

An electric fence is unsightly. Since I was running it through my garden railway, I wanted a system that I could pick up at will for open houses, then easily replace. I installed steel stakes, the type used to build concrete forms. These are solid, round rods with a point at one end. I liked them for their strength. Since the wire must be insulated from ground, I ran it through ½" PVC pipe and "Ts." The pipe is slid over the steel stakes and serves as a spacer to make it the right height and to insulate the wire from the metal stake, while the PVC "T" is used to hold the wire. I first drilled holes in the stem of the "T," then ran the wire through the hole. This worked just fine, but threading the wire through the hole was a lot of work. To make it easier, I installed small metal eyes, with the eye opened slightly at the bottom so the wire can be hooked and led into the eye. This made installation and removal much quicker.

I started out with steel stakes for their extra strength, as I had to bang the stake into the ground. For installation in softer ground, I made lighter-duty stakes from sprinkler sticks. You could also make stakes out of PVC pipe. Holes can be drilled into the pipe and a cotter key used to hold the wire.

After installing and taking down the electric wire a half-dozen times, I realized this was a lot of work and that the steel rods were heavy to carry. For a permanent installation, the above system works well. However, I needed a more portable system, so I came up with the following: Since I can't pound PVC pipe into the ground, I set up sockets. In place of the steel rods, I installed a foot-long piece of 1" PVC, pushed into the hole down to ground level to form a socket. Then I dropped an 18" piece of ½" PVC into the hole, so that about 6" is above ground. I pre-drilled the pipe with several sets of holes that could be used to alter the height of the wire. Next, I strung the wire using cotter pins. I ran the wire through the eye of each cotter pin and installed the pin in the proper hole. I have found this to be a quick and easy system to set up and remove.

A side benefit of an electric fence is that my pond has stayed cleaner longer. Much of the debris was due to animals digging around the water and pushing dirt into the pond.

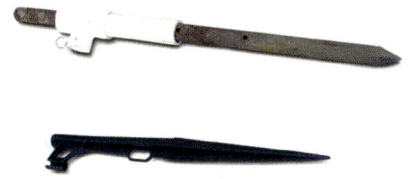

Stakes for the fence. The bottom stake is a plastic sprinkler stick with an eye screw, through which the wire is passed. This can be used in light-duty applications. At top is a steel rod, which must be hammered into the ground. A PVC pipe "T" and pipe is slipped over the stake and used as a spacer and insulator.

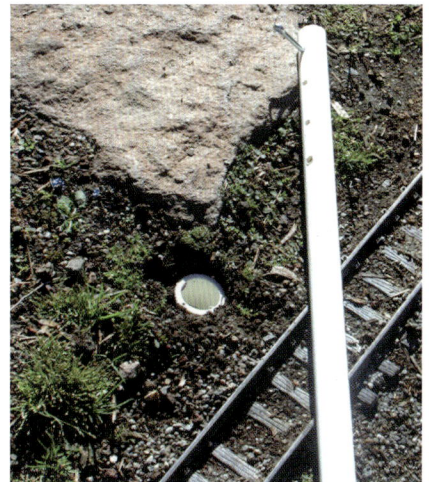

This is my installation, designed to be quickly removed and replaced. A 12"-long piece of 1" PVC pipe is driven into the ground as the socket. The ½" pipe on the right is installed by dropping it into the socket.

Here the stake has been installed in its socket. The wire is held in place by a cotter pin. A hook or eye could also be used to hold the wire.

Suppliers

Chapter 3

Richard Hillman Rail Clamps
P.O. Box 1253
Lodi, CA 95241
209-369-1868
www.hillmansrailclamps.com

PVC pipe, ½", schedule 40:
Plumbing store, building supply
store, hardware store

Chapter 5

Kadee Quality Products Co.
673 Avenue C
White City, OR 97503-1078
541-826-3883
www.kadee.com

Gary Raymond
P.O. Box 1722
Thousand Oaks, CA 91358
805-492-5858
www.trainwheels.com

San Val
7444 Valjean Ave.
Van Nuys, CA 91406
800-423-3281
www.san-val.com

Micro torch: hobby shop,
hardware store
Rosin-core solder: Hardware
store, electronics store

Chapter 7

Miniature Plant Kingdom
4125 Harrison Grade Rd.
Sebastopol, CA 95472
707-874-2233

Durarock: lumber yard, home
center, building supply store

Chapter 8

Aquascape
www.aquascapedesigns.com

Cal Pump
28606 W. Livingston Ave.
Valencia, CA 91355
800-225-1339
www.calpump.com

Dow Products
800-800-3626
www.dow.com/
buildingproducts/enerfoam/
index.htm

12" diameter corrugated
plastic drain pipe: irrigation
supply house

MEK: hardware store,
paint store

Tetra Sales USA
3001 Commerce St.
Blacksburg, VA 24060
800-423-6458
www.tetra-fish.com

Chapter 9

**Fountain Care Anti-Foam
Aquarium Pharmaceuticals, Inc.**
P.O. Box 218
Chalfont, PA 18914-0218
215-822-8181
www.petsforum.com/aqharm

Garden Works
13215 S.E. 30th
Bellevue, WA 98005
425-455-0568
aquariumpharm.com

**Scare Crow
Contech Electronics**
6582 Bryn Rd.
Victoria, BC V8M 1X6
Canada
800-767-8658
www.scatmat.com

Zareba Systems
906 Fifth Ave. E.
Ellendale, MN 56026
507-684-3721
www.zarebasystems.com

Large-scale train manufacturers

Aristo-Craft Trains
698 S. 21st St.
Irvington, NJ 07111-4109
973-351-9800
www.aristocraft.com

Accucraft AMS
33268 Central Ave.
Union City, CA 94587
510-324-3399
www.amstrains.com

Bachmann Industries, Inc.
1400 E. Erie Ave.
Philadelphia, PA 19124
215-533-1600
www.bachmanntrains.com

Hartford Products, Inc.
P.O. Box 553
King City, MO 64463
660-535-6362
www.hartfordpr.com

Hartland Locomotive Works
P.O. Box 1743
Laporte, IN 46352

219-362-8411
www.H-L-W.com

LGB of America
6444 Nancy Ridge Dr.
San Diego, CA 92121
800-669-0607
www.lgb.com

MTH Electric Trains
7020 Columbia Gateway Dr.
Columbia, MD 21046
410-381-2580
www.mthtrains.com

USA Trains
P.O. Box 100
Malden, MA 02148
781-322-6084
www.usatrains.com

Suppliers

Big Train Backshop
P.O. Box 991
San Luis Obispo, CA
93406-0991
805-541-0546
slotrains@charter.net
Details, figures, model kits

Bragdon Enterprises
2960 Garden Tower Ln.
Georgetown, CA 95634
530-333-1365
www.bragdonent.com
Rock molds

Bridgemasters
1077 Promenade Ave.
Placentia, CA 93870
714-985-9007
www.bridge-masters.com
Bridges and accessories

Bridgewerks
126 Hunt St.
Durham, NC 27701
714-337-0722
www.bridgewerks.com
Model railroad power supplies

**California & Oregon Coast
Railway**
P.O. Box 57
Rouge River, OR 97537
800-866-8635
www.cocry.com
E-Z Air turnout components

Custom Model Products
1070 Shary Circle
Concord, CA 94518
925-687-3500
www.custommodelproducts.com
Locomotives, freight cars

Dallee Electronics, Inc.
246 W. Main St.
Leola, PA 17540
717-661-7041
www.dallee.com
Sound systems, electronics

Eaglewings Iron Craft
1522 E. Victory, Ste. 1
Phoenix, AZ 85040
602-276-8101
www.eaglewingsironcraft.com
Metal bridges

Evergreen Scale Models, Inc.
18620-F 141st Ave. N.E.
Woodinville, WA 98072
425-402-4918
www.evergreenscalemodels.com
Plastic sheets and shapes

Fall Creek Railroad
P.O. Box 191636, Dept. BTS
Sacramento, CA 95819
916-383-6001
www.g-scale.com/g-scale/
Exhibitors/FallCreek.html
Turntables and structures

Grandt Line Products
1040-B Shary Ct.
Concord, CA 94518
www.grandtline.com
Scale doors and windows

Jameco Electronics
1355 Shoreway Rd.
Belmont, CA 94002
800-237-6948
www.jameco.com
Electronics

Just Plain Folk
818 Lincoln Ave.
Palmyra, NJ 08065
865-786-0080
www.trackntrains.com
Figures and details

Lone Star Bridge & Abutment
410 Lillard, No. 206
Arlington, TX 76012
888-548-5656
www.lonestarbridge.com
Bridges

Micro-Mark
340 Snyder Ave.
Berkeley Heights, NJ 07922
908-464-2984
www.micromark.com
Model making tools

Miniature Plant Kingdom
1340 Harrison Grade Pl.
Sebastopol, CA 95472
www.miniplantkingdom.com
Plants

Mini Forest by Sky
P.O. Box 1156
Mulino, Oregon 97042
503-632-3555
www.miniforest.com
Miniature plants

Northwest Remote Control
425-823-3507
dnkgoods.home.mindspring.com
Battery remote controls

Ozark Miniatures Inc.
3461 S. 5225 W.
Cedar City, UT 84720
435-586-1036
www.ozarkminiatures.com
Cast metal detail parts and
accessories

**Pacific Coast Garden
Railway Supply**
Randy D. Bryie
12081 Pradera Rd.
Camarillo, CA 93012
mysite.verizon.net/bryie/pcgrs
Structures

Phoenix Sound Systems, Inc.
3514 W. Liberty Rd.
Ann Arbor, MI 48103
800-651-2444
www.phoenixsound.com
Sound systems

Radio Shack
800-843-7422
www.radioshack.com

Railroad Ave.
P.O. Box 550
Willits, CA 95490
707-459-2770
www.railroadavenue.com
Resin model railroad structures

Ram Track
229 E. Rollins Rd.
Round Lake Beach, IL 60073
847-740-8726
www.ramrcandramtrack.com
Sound units, electronic devices

Soundtraxx
210 Rock Point Dr.
Durango, CO 81301
970-259-0690
www.soundtraxx.com
Sound systems

Stanley & Sons Nursery
11740 S.E. Orient Dr.
Boring, OR 97009
800-805-9157
www.stanleyandsons.com
Plants

Sunset Valley Railroad
21616 23rd St. Ct. E
Bonney Lake, WA 98391
253-862-6748
www.svrronline.com
Track and turnouts

Track 'n Trains
111 W. Broad St.
Palmyra, NJ 08065
www.trackntrains.com
Scale figures and accessories